BEYOND INTIFADA

BEYOND INTIFADA

Narratives of Freedom Fighters in the Gaza Strip

Haim Gordon, Rivca Gordon, and Taher Shriteh

Westport, Connecticut
London

Library of Congress Cataloging-in-Publication Data

Gordon, Hayim.
    Beyond intifada : narratives of freedom fighters in the Gaza Strip / Haim
  Gordon, Rivca Gordon, and Taher Shriteh.
      p.   cm.
  Includes bibliographical references and index.
  ISBN 0–275–97129–5 (alk. paper)
    1. Al-Aqsa Intifada, 2000—Personal narratives, Palestinian Arab.   I. Gordon,
  Rivca.   II. Shriteh, Taher.   III. Title.
  DS119.765 .G67 2003
  956.95'3044—dc21   2002028764

British Library Cataloguing in Publication Data is available.

Library of Congress Catalog Card Number: 2002028764
ISBN: 0–275–97129–5

First published in 2003

Praeger Publishers, 88 Post Road West, Westport, CT 06881
An imprint of Greenwood Publishing Group, Inc.
www.praeger.com

Printed in the United States of America

The paper used in this book complies with the
Permanent Paper Standard issued by the National
Information Standards Organization (Z39.48–1984).

10 9 8 7 6 5 4 3 2 1

Contents

Introduction

Today the exciting story of the intifada that began in 1987 in the Gaza Strip and the inspiring and sad outcomes of this story are slowly fading from the collective consciousness of the world. In the last weeks of 1987, however, this small strip of land became the major battleground upon which was initiated and took place one of the few national rebellions of the second half of the twentieth century. By throwing stones, burning tires, marching, and demonstrating, Palestinian youths and teenagers demanded an end to the Israeli military occupation of the Gaza Strip and the West Bank. These young people declared that they were struggling for freedom, for dignity, and for justice. They continued their struggle for months, for six years. After the first few days of the youth rebellion, the generation of their fathers and mothers slowly joined them; but during all the years of the intifada the youths were usually the spearhead of the Palestinian struggle for freedom.

The Israeli army responded to the intifada with beatings, tear gas, and bullets, as well as with curfews, the closing of schools and universities, and widespread arrests, torture, and what international observers called kangaroo trials. To no avail. The rebellion refused to disappear. It finally led to at least a partial understanding within Israel that the Palestinians deserved a state of their own, that the Israeli military occupation of the Gaza Strip and the West Bank was wrong, and that Israel should not occupy the Gaza Strip. Consequently, in 1993 a peace process was initiated. After a few months, Israel seemingly evacuated the Gaza Strip. A few months later, Yasser Arafat, the leader of the Palestine Liberation Organization (PLO), set up the offices of the Palestinian Authority in Gaza City. The intifada ended after it seemed to have attained its declared goal.

The following pages suggest that the situation is much more complex and that the freedom fighters in the Gaza Strip believe that their goals are far from being realized. This sad outcome emerges slowly as the reader progresses from chapter to chapter. On the whole, this book constitutes one of the first attempts to present a personal and social history of some of the less well-known people in the Gaza Strip who participated in the intifada. Although quite a few published books have described the intifada, or various aspects of it, a personal and social history of this rebellion has not been published. What is more, the history of the Gaza Strip has only rarely been addressed by the scholarly community.

We repeat: As the following personal testimonies indicate, and as many daily mundane facts reveal, few of the goals of the intifada have been attained. Israeli military occupation of the Gaza Strip is still a fact of life. Palestinians frequently announce that Israeli exploitation and oppression of the residents of the Gaza Strip continue to ruin their lives. They repeatedly state that the Israeli army continues to perform evil deeds against the Palestinians whom it rules. Freedom, dignity, and justice for the Palestinians living in the Gaza Strip, they admit, is still a remote dream.

One can still ask: What do you mean by justice in that troubled area of the world? For what just causes are the Israelis who support freedom for the Palestinians and the Palestinian people struggling?

Answers to these questions appear later in the book, often in a subtle and rather roundabout manner. Hence, here we will provide some of the ideas that underlie our understanding of how Israel should respond to the Palestinian struggle for freedom, for justice, and for dignity. We should add that these ideas often have been brought up in the Israeli Knesset by Knesset members who belong to Israeli political parties that support peace and justice with the Palestinians. (The Knesset members who belong to these parties constitute almost a quarter of the Knesset.)

Here is a brief and immediately relevant list of the ideas, suggested by these Israeli Knesset members on various occasions; they and we believe that these ideas will help to ensure freedom, justice, and dignity for the Palestinian people. The list includes the following demands from Israel: return of Israeli military forces to the 1967 borders and the establishment of a Palestinian State on the land of historical Palestine, including Jerusalem; respect of the freedom and human rights of Palestinians; a halt to Israeli economic exploitation of Palestinian society; Israel's sharing of natural resources such as water with the Palestinians; diminishment of the political role of the military in Israeli and Palestinian society; the return of Palestinian land in the Gaza Strip, that was confiscated by Israel, to its owners; freedom of movement for Palestinians and their goods; establishment of Israeli-Palestinian joint projects to protect the environment; and dialogue on educational and cultural topics.

We submit that these ideas and requirements are hardly complex. As the Israeli Knesset members who discussed these ideas often explained, the ideas are found at the basis of any enlightened understanding of the ways of life in a democratic society. Yet many Israeli politicians and citizens refuse to acknowledge that these ideas and requirements should serve as the foundation of Israel's relations to the Palestinian people.

This book has been researched and written by two Israelis, Rivca Gordon and Haim Gordon, and a Palestinian, Taher Shriteh. We worked together willingly and with full trust, despite the harsh political and personal circumstances of the Palestinians, which serve as the background for the following testimonies. We recognize that the following chapters can only partially uncover the truths about the difficult personal and social history of the Palestinians in the Gaza Strip during the second half of the twentieth century—difficulties that continue today.

We believe that the process of bringing this book to publication is part of our struggle for the freedom and dignity of the Palestinian people and for justice toward them. It is also part of our struggle to build genuine neighborly relations between Israelis and Palestinians—relations that suggest that Israelis and Palestinians can live side by side as good neighbors in two separate states. To show the links of this book to our everyday concerns and to our struggle for justice, we have included a background chapter describing the personal involvement of Rivca Gordon and Haim Gordon in what has been happening in the Gaza Strip. Also, Taher Shriteh is among the freedom fighters whose narratives constitute the major section of this book. Thus we have blended our personal stories with the stories and descriptions of some of the struggles for freedom undertaken by the Palestinians in the Gaza Strip.

The value of our research and writing will be decided by history. Yet already, in the introduction, one conclusion can be stated. With all due modesty, we believe that the book is at least a partial triumph in the quest for trust and dialogue between Israelis and Palestinians. This difficult quest has been part of our lives for many years. Our desire to respond to the challenge of this quest was one of the reasons that we embarked on researching and writing this personal and social history of the intifada in the Gaza Strip. The book is a testimony to the fact that even in adverse and horrendous circumstances, which are politically destructive of freedom and dignity, even when evil policies and deeds prevail, the struggle for dialogue, for truth, and for justice can bear fruit. The chapter on Taher Shriteh and the chapter on Rivca Gordon and Haim Gordon, we believe, add to the atmosphere of dialogue that this book wishes to promote.

It should already be evident that we authors want justice to prevail and want the Israeli and the Palestinian peoples to learn to live together as neighbors in this area of the world. Dialogue and trust are necessary for such goals to be attained. But the situation in which we exist is also circular. An authentic struggle for justice and freedom, undertaken by Israelis and Palestinians working together, can help to establish dialogue and trust between them.

Personal narratives of four Palestinian men and two Palestinian women are central to our descriptions of the plight of the Palestinians in the Gaza Strip, the intifada, and the beginning of the so-called peace process. We agree that some of the narratives and some of the views expressed by the narrators may be problematic and unacceptable to some readers. Yet these views are a testimony to the complexity of life in the Gaza Strip and are true to the political and religious spectrum of ideas that prevails there.

It should be clear, however, that the following pages are not an exercise in postmodern narrative-oriented history. We cannot present here in any depth our firm rejection of the superficiality and inanity that emanate from many postmodern approaches and writings. In the current context, we can say that we especially condemn the postmodern attempts to spread ethical relativism and to explain away blatant evils.

We also reject the postmodern explanation that reduces events, including many evils, to cultural trends. Evil must not be explained or redeemed, as Sartre once noted, evil must be fought—daily. Hence, we scorn the postmodern attempt to create a halo around every narrative, even if the narrative stinks of deceit and bad faith.[1] In short, we have learned that many, if not most, postmodern approaches are an assault on truth and a flight from the responsibility for the many evils that exist in the world that we share with others. We condemn such an assault on truth and, with it, the postmodern flight from responsibility.

Hence, the six narratives that are central to this book should be viewed as what they are: the personal stories of the lives of six Palestinians who fought for freedom from Israeli military rule before and during the intifada. Each Palestinian related crucial events in his or her life story to us. In hearing these stories and posing questions, we did not follow a fixed format. We let the narrator lead the way. Thus, there are narrators who spoke little about their personal and family life, while others spoke at length on these topics. We recorded these stories as they were presented. Of course, we edited repetitious and irrelevant statements, but we made no changes in the text. We recorded these narratives not only in order to show some of the personally destructive aspects of Israel's continual military occupation of the Gaza Strip, but also to honor all the Palestinians residing in the Gaza Strip by indicating that they also have a place in history. They have a story that is worthy of being told.

Learning from Hannah Arendt, we can state that the six narratives are life stories that disclose, at least partially, the *who* of each of the six Palestinian narrators. Arendt distinguishes between *what* a person is—a plumber, a truckdriver, a mother, a professor, a political leader—and *who* that person is as a unique human being. She explains that *what* a person is can be described by a concept or a group of concepts. In order to know *who* a person is, however, the person must tell at least part of his or her life story.

We believe that future historians will learn from the *who* of the Palestinians who narrate the stories of their struggle for freedom against Israeli military rule. We believe that such historians will relate with respect to the elements of the historical truth about the Palestinian struggle for freedom that emerge in these narratives. We hold these beliefs because the narratives in this book have an independence of their own; they express the unique being of each Palestinian. These unique expressions of human existence will continue to assist their readers, as they helped us, to learn truths and reach conclusions.

The book is divided into three sections. The first section gives some background to the narratives that follow. We first present a short overview of the Gaza Strip as a geographical, political, historical, economic entity. We describe some of the characteristics of the Israeli military rule in the Gaza Strip. We then describe the involvement of Rivca Gordon and Haim Gordon in working for human rights in the Gaza Strip.

The second section, which constitutes the major thrust of this book, presents the narratives of the six freedom fighters. In the narratives, each freedom fighter describes his or her struggle for freedom in his or her own terms. We hope that the throbbing life of this struggle for freedom emerges in these pages.

Our conception of the third section of this book changed while we were working on it. When we conceived this book and began our research, we believed and hoped that we were on the road to a just peace between Israel and the Palestinian people. We were dead wrong. Israel's policies and deeds during the seven years of the interim period defined by the establishers of the peace process led to a new intifada. What is worse, in response to the new intifada, Intifadet El Aqsa, that erupted on September 28, 2000, Israel began a series of steps that culminated in its armed forces committing grave deeds against the Palestinian people. According to definitions agreed upon by the International Criminal Court under the United Nations, some of Israel's grave deeds should be called war crimes.

We were faced with a problem. We had completed gathering the narratives in the late spring of 2000. While we were transcribing, editing, and preparing the book for publication, the entire area had exploded again. How should we complete this book, especially since Intifadet El Aqsa erupted after all of the narratives had been gathered?

After some thought, we decided to leave the narratives as they were presented. We decided not to ask the narrators for additional material, nor did we want to analyze the narratives. We felt that the power of the narratives was in their presentation of a personal testimony, in their description of each narrator's personal contribution to a crucial moment in the history of the Palestinian people.

But we did not want to gloss over the new situation that has been created by the eruption of Intifadet El Aqsa. Consequently, in the third section we described Israel's deeds that, according to Palestinian sources, contributed to the eruption of the new intifada. We also chose to describe some of Israel's harsh deeds against the Palestinian people that can be termed war crimes according to the definition of a war crime formulated by the International Criminal Court under the United Nations. These war crimes have been condemned by some Israeli journalists writing in the Israeli press, in addition to being denounced in the international press. These deeds, we explain, are being committed against the Palestinian people, in response to Intifadet El Aqsa, by forces under the command of Major General Shaul Mufaz, the chief of staff of the Israel Defense Forces.

In Chapter 9, we describe the new intifada and point out some of these war crimes. We conclude that the Palestinians are correct in stating that today Israel's overall purpose in the Gaza Strip is to strangle the Palestinian quest for freedom. Many leading Israeli politicians do not challenge this view. From our acquaintance with the situation, which includes what we learned from the testimonies of the six freedom fighters that appear in this book, we have grave doubts that Israel's political acts will succeed in smothering the Palestinian struggle for freedom.

We did not want to end this book on a pessimistic note. Hence, the final chapter is dedicated to a short discussion of the sources of hope for Palestinian freedom and for a just and lasting peace.

NOTE

1. For an example of the stupidities emerging in much postmodern writing, see: Haim Gordon, review of *Terror in the Mind of God: The Global Rise of Religious Violence*, by Mark Juergensmeyer, Global Dialogue 2, no. 3 (2000): 152–157.

Part 1

Background

Chapter 1

The Gaza Strip: An Overview

The Gaza Strip is approximately forty-six kilometers long. It is approximately eight kilometers wide. Its total area is 360 square kilometers. To the north and the east the Gaza Strip borders Israel. To the south it borders Egypt. To the west is the Mediterranean Sea.

Today the Gaza Strip is surrounded by a high fence which day and night is patrolled and guarded on the northern and eastern borders by Israeli troops, and by Israeli and Egyptian soldiers on the southern border. The Mediterranean Sea is patrolled by Israeli Dabur gunboats. There are only five official entrances to the Gaza Strip. Karni passage is for transferring goods to and from Israel. Palestinians can use only the Erez entrance in order to enter Israel and the Rafah entrance in order to enter Egypt. The other two entrances are for Israelis, mainly settlers. The Israel Defense Forces in conjunction with the Israeli security service, the Shabak, decide who among Israelis and Palestinians is permitted to use these entrances, including the entrance to Egypt; they also decide when that person is allowed to use these entrances.

The Gaza Strip was established as a political and geographical entity in 1948, following the first Arab-Israeli war. That war was a result of the decision of the Arab nations bordering Palestine and of many of the Arabs living in Palestine to fight against the United Nations decision to establish a Jewish State on part of the land that had been the British Mandate in Palestine. These nations notified the world that they would annihilate the Jewish State if it were established when the British Mandate terminated. True to their word, five Arab armies began to invade Israel on May 15, 1948, when the British Mandate in Palestine ended and the British troops evacuated the area. These invading armies were supported by some of the Palestinian Arabs living in Palestine.

Israel's declaration of independence was signed by its representatives in Tel Aviv on May 15, 1948. Hence, the establishment of Israel and its recognition as an independent state after its army defeated the invading Arab armies more or less coincided with the creation of the Gaza Strip as a political entity. During the 1948 War, approximately 250,000 Arabs who resided in the south of Palestine fled from their homes to the Gaza Strip, altering the demographic and social structure of the area. This alteration was significant in the decision to recognize the Gaza Strip as an unique political entity. Other Arab refugees fled from other parts of Israel to neighboring countries such as Lebanon, Syria, and Jordan.

When the 1948 War ended, an extended cease-fire was negotiated and finally signed by the parties to the conflict. According to the cease-fire agreements, the Gaza Strip came under Egyptian military rule. For the next nineteen years, Egyptian rulers accepted that situation and did little to improve the plight of the residents of the Gaza Strip.

The Egyptian military administration which ruled the Gaza Strip gave some rights to the Palestinians residing in the territory, but definitely not the rights of Egyptian citizenship. We should add that following the 1948 War, all of the Arab states refused to absorb the Palestinians who had become refugees. The Arab League also decreed that Palestinian refugees could not become citizens of the countries in which they resided. Israel also refused to allow the refugees to return to their homes within the newly established state of Israel. This political disagreement resulted in the Palestinian refugees being stateless, doomed to exist in their refugee camps or as noncitizens in their countries of refuge.

The immediate consequences of these political decisions for all of the people living in the Gaza Strip were horrendous. Together with the refugees, all the indigenous residents of the Gaza Strip, who had lived in the area for generations, had suddenly become stateless persons in their undeveloped, newly created political entity. They soon learned that they were merely pawns in a major Middle East political conflict.

For decades, the main money-making agricultural crop in the Gaza Strip was citrus fruits for export. Prior to 1948 the area that became the Gaza Strip had not been a center of economic activity. After the influx of refugees and under Egyptian rule, there was little promotion of economic opportunity or development of infrastructure. Poverty and abandonment very much characterized the area.

The Gaza Strip came under Israeli military occupation during the June 1967 war between Israel and the combined armies of Egypt, Syria, and Jordan. Israel won that war and occupied the Sinai Peninsula, the Gaza Strip, the West Bank of the Jordan, and the Syrian Golan Heights. Since then the Gaza Strip has been under Israeli military occupation. Although Israel has been a democracy with freedom of speech and political activity for almost three decades, the Israeli army ruled the Gaza Strip by military decree and prohibited all Palestinian political activity. Quite often the Israeli military issued decrees that trampled upon the human rights of the Palestinians living in the Gaza Strip.

Here is just one example. Under Israeli military rule, as under Egyptian military rule, the Palestinian residents of the Gaza Strip were regarded as stateless.

They had no passports and were given no civil or political rights. In the 1990s, a small number of Palestinians were given magnetic cards which allowed them to cross the border and enter Israel. The main reason Palestinians wished to enter Israel was in order to find work. Those who could not get a magnetic card were confined to living in the Gaza Strip for their entire lives.

On May 18, 1994, the Palestinian Authority entered the Gaza Strip under the leadership of Yasser Arafat and the Palestine Liberation Organization (PLO). Arafat himself entered the Gaza Strip on July 1, 1994. But according to the initial agreement between the PLO and Israel during the period that was called the interim stage, from 1993 to 1999, the Palestinian Authority received very little political power. The interim stage did not end at its announced date, May 1999, and Israel is still, today, politically responsible for what occurs in the Gaza Strip. The Israeli military is the absolute ruler in the realms of security, foreign policy, and economic policy.

During the twenty-eight years of Israeli direct military rule very little statistical research was conducted as to the conditions in the Gaza Strip. Hence, some of the following statistical statements are approximations.

Today the Israeli army continues to rule the Gaza Strip as an occupied military zone. The entry of the PLO into the Gaza Strip in 1994 and the establishment of what is called the Palestinian Authority under the leadership of President Yasser Arafat—both of which occurred during the first stages of the 1993 peace process—did not alter the basic situation whereby Israel rules the area by military decree. Nor did these actions diminish Israeli oppression and exploitation of the residents of the Gaza Strip. The fact that past and present Israeli policies have created a situation whereby, according to Palestinian sources, around 85 percent of the Palestinians residing in the Gaza Strip do not have freedom of movement is a notable example of Israel's harsh military rule.

Look at this fact closely. It is an accepted fact that 1.1 million Palestinians reside today in the Gaza Strip. It is the most densely populated area on the face of the earth. Over 70 percent of the population of the Gaza Strip are refugees or the descendents of refugees of the 1948 War with Israel. According to the United Nations, 818,000 of the residents of the Gaza Strip are refugees or their descendents. The average number of childen in a refugee family, again according to the United Nations, is 7.5. Consequently, half of the Palestinian refugees residing in the Gaza Strip are under the age of fifteen. The eight refugee camps that were set up in the Gaza Strip in 1948 serve as home to approximately 465,000 Palestinians. Almost all these people are stuck in deep poverty and degrading squalor. All of them are still partially supported economically by the United Nations Relief and Works Agency for Palestinian Refugees (UNRWA). UNRWA periodically awards all these refugees small grants of food and is responsible for initial medical treatment for the refugees, elementary and middle schooling, and other assistances.

As we indicated, almost all of the residents of the Gaza Strip are directly or indirectly denied freedom of movement by the Israeli military. Although there are no published statistics about the Israeli limitations on the freedom of movement of the Palestinians, it is safe to say that no more than 15 percent of the residents of the Gaza Strip can leave it. At least 900,000 Palestinians are condemned to live in this dismal, crowded, impoverished ghetto—many Palestinians call it a cage.

Consider these Palestinian refugees. They or their parents or grandparents fled more than half a century ago into the Gaza Strip. Since then all members of the family are confined to this tiny, overpopulated area. These refugees and their progeny have no possibility of traveling to another area of the world, including the close Palestinian area of the West Bank or neighboring countries such as Israel, Jordan, or Egypt. For many of the refugees, Europe is beyond their furthest horizon.

The two reasons for this restriction upon Palestinian freedom of movement are both outcomes of Israeli policy since 1967. The first reason is the widespread poverty in the Gaza Strip which is a direct result of Israeli military decisions. This reason deserves to be explained in some detail.

Central to Israel's military rule of the Palestinians in the Gaza Strip was the political decision not to allow any substantial economic development in the area. To be specific, no major international or local investments in medium or large industrial enterprises were allowed in the Gaza Strip. Due to this decision, the Gaza Strip was barren of economic opportunities for almost all of its residents.

Until the eruption of the intifada, the Palestinians from the Gaza Strip who sought work were incorporated as cheap laborers in the Israeli economy. They worked within Israel in agriculture, industry, construction, and the service sector as dishwashers and at other menial jobs. When the demand for Palestinian laborers was at its peak, close to 70,000 approved laborers traveled daily from the Gaza Strip to work in Israel, returning to their homes at night. At most, there were another 35,000 Palestinian laborers from the Gaza Strip who were working in Israel illegally. It is evident that allowing the residents of the Gaza Strip to work in Israel for low wages while not allowing any industrial development within the Gaza Strip is not a way to further economic development.

We wish to repeat this major point. During its twenty-eight years of direct military rule, Israel decided that there would be no opportunities for economic development in the Gaza Strip. What is more, the officers in the Israeli military regime in the Gaza Strip linked their giving a Palestinian a minor economic opportunity—say, to open a gas station or purchase a fax machine—to the Palestinian's implicit and explicit support of Israel's continual military rule. In short, as the following testimonies repeatedly reveal, Palestinian collaborators were given limited economic opportunity; they were also allowed more freedom of movement.

This policy had grave economic outcomes for the large majority of residents in the Gaza Strip. In her fine book, *The Gaza Strip: The Political Economy of De-development*, Sara Roy has meticulously shown many of the details of Israel's purposeful de-development of the Gaza Strip, a policy which has continued for the past three and a half decades.[1]

An additional result of Israel's decision to block economic development was the lack of Israeli investment in the infrastructure of the Gaza Strip: roads, sewage systems, housing, communication networks, hospitals, or schools. This situation only began to change when the Palestinian Authority took over in 1994 and received some international aid for repairing the terrible sewage system and the run-down roads and for beginning to build a modern infrastructure. Consequently, Israel's oppressive economic policy is responsible for the poverty and squalor that abounds throughout the Gaza Strip and especially in the lives of the Palestinian refugees. As mentioned, this abject poverty gravely limits the freedom of movement of the population. To give an example, a family of eight that lives on $300 a month, which is a very common situation, has no funds for travel. And there are many large families in the Gaza Strip who have an even smaller monthly income.

The second reason that Israel states for its refusal to allow Palestinians residing in the Gaza Strip freedom of movement is termed "security reasons." We hold this second reason to be dubious at best. At least 850,000 of the 900,000 Palestinians who will never have the funds or will never be allowed to travel outside the Gaza Strip are definitely *not* terrorists. Why are they denied freedom of movement, even into Israel?

We believe that the fundamental reason for this denial of freedom of movement—which political philosopher Hannah Arendt has called the most basic of freedoms—is that Israeli military authorities recognize, correctly, that freedom of movement would slowly erode the possibility of enforcing the military occupation of the Gaza Strip that currently prevails.

Gaza City in the north of the Gaza Strip has a population of more than 300,000; it is the largest city in the Gaza Strip and the center of political and economic activity. There are only two other major cities. Khan Yunis is in the center of the Gaza Strip, with a population of approximately 200,000. Rafah is at the southern end and borders Egypt; it has approximately 120,000 residents. In addition, the Gaza Strip has around forty townships and recognized communities.

As indicated, the majority of the refugees in the Gaza Strip live in eight overcrowded refugee camps. They live in extreme poverty and deplorable conditions. One must remember, however, that in 1948 there were some Palestinian refugees who came to the Gaza Strip with financial means and some who had marketable skills. These means and skills allowed them to establish homes outside the refugee camps. Since 1948, thousands of additional refugee families have found the financial means to get out of the degrading life that prevails in the refugee camps.

In addition to the refugees from the 1948 War and their progeny, the current population of the Gaza Strip includes descendents of the indigenous Gazan families who resided in the area before 1948; there are also descendents of the

Bedouin tribes and the Bedouin extended families who grazed their flocks in the southern parts of Palestine during the British Mandate. Among the indigenous Gazans, there is a tiny minority of Christians who reside in the Gaza Strip—an island of Christianity in the sea of Islam. Today, many of the families of the indigenous Gazans constitute the economic and political elite. These families own much land and have been financially established in the area for generations.

In 1948, many of the Bedouins who lived in the southern area of Palestine, the Negev, fled to the Gaza Strip; they became refugees. There were, however, certain Bedouin tribes and extended families who had owned land in the Gaza Strip prior to 1948. Their status differed substantially from the other Bedouin tribes who fled or were forced to flee to the Gaza Strip and hence became refugees. Some of the descendents of those Bedouin tribes and families who owned land in the Gaza Strip have settled on their land and till it; others have become city dwellers and have joined the economic and political elite. Some of the Bedouins differ a bit from other Gazans in their culture and tribal and family structure. Many of these Bedouins still accept the mores and norms of nomads. However, there are Bedouin families who are slowly becoming urbanized.

Despite the harsh conditions that have prevailed in the Gaza Strip during the past half century, particularly in the refugee camps—or perhaps because of these harsh conditions—education, including education for girls, has been a top priority for almost all residents of the Gaza Strip. The facts that there were very few school buildings and that learning in elementary school was in two or three shifts did not diminish the value of education for the Palestinians residing in the Gaza Strip. Anywhere in the Gaza Strip in the hour between the school shifts, thousands of elementary school boys and girls, dressed in their school uniforms and holding satchels, can be seen walking to and from school.

Learning was also difficult for the pupils in the Gaza Strip because many school classes had no less than fifty pupils. Furthermore, for many years there were very few certified teachers. Still, it would be safe to say that today more than 90 percent of the children in the Gaza Strip attend school regularly, and the large majority of these children acquire basic learning skills. Close to 70 percent of the pupils continue to secondary school. Today, when there are two universities in Gaza City and other institutions of higher learning in the Gaza Strip, around 50 percent of the graduates of secondary school seek higher education in teacher seminars or universities.

During the past half century many Palestinian youths in the Gaza Strip excelled in their studies, especially since excelling in learning was and is highly valued by Palestinian society. Some of these stateless people, and especially many of the refugees and their descendents, viewed obtaining a good education as one of the few ways to flee their oppressive situation. They believed that it might assist the educated person to perhaps obtain a good paying job in an Arab country or maybe even in Europe.

In the past three and a half decades, many of those young people who excelled in secondary schools in the Gaza Strip have sought to continue their educations at the university level. Since until the early 1990s there were few opportunities for higher education in the Gaza Strip, many Palestinian secondary school graduates studied at universities in Arab countries such as Egypt, Libya, Tunisia, and Iraq. Quite a few also enrolled in universities in Europe and North America. After graduating and obtaining high academic degrees, however, few of those who studied in Europe and North America have returned to the Gaza Strip. There are no precise figures about this nonreturn of Palestinian graduates. Yet it is safe to assume that during this past half century many thousands of Palestinian graduates have found ways to remain in Europe and North America.

We believe that there are two major reasons that lead Palestinian university graduates in Europe and North America to decide not to return to the Gaza Strip. One reason is that during their years of study, these young Palestinian graduates have become accustomed to living in a society characterized by political freedom. They do not want to return to live in an area that is harshly ruled by the Israeli military. Who wants to live as a second-class citizen in the world?

Another reason is that for almost three decades the ruling Israeli military purposely did not allow any political, cultural, or economic development to occur in the Gaza Strip. Consequently, during these years there were very few jobs available for Palestinians with advanced academic degrees. Most of those university graduates who did return to the Gaza Strip did not find work in their field. It is not exceptional, even today, to find a Palestinian university graduate who boasts a degree in economics, English literature, or modern history working as an agricultural laborer or in construction.

Since 1967, Israel has confiscated approximately 35 percent of the land of the Gaza Strip, much of it prime agricultural land. On this confiscated land, Israel set up nineteen Jewish settlements. Official statistics announce that the settlements in the Gaza Strip are home to 6,000 Israeli citizens. However, according to the Israeli press, at least a third of the so-called settlers in the Gaza Strip do not reside in the settlements. They acquired a so-called home in a settlement as an investment or as a political act which adds support to their view that Israel has the right to settle upon that land.

Many of the Jewish settlers who do reside in the Gaza Strip received Israeli government interest-free loans to set up advanced agricultural projects on the land that was confiscated from Palestinians. Most of these agricultural enterprises are labor intensive—say, greenhouses for export crops, or raising organic vegetables for both the Israeli market and export. The settlers employ impoverished Palestinians from the Gaza Strip as laborers in these agricultural projects. At times, these are the same Palestinians who were forcefully evicted from the land upon which the settlers set up their money-making projects. These Palestinian laborers receive wages that are much lower than the lawful minimum wage given to laborers in Israel. In addition, these Palestinian laborers are not awarded the social benefits that Israeli law awards to all laborers.

Palestinian spokespersons and lay people have repeatedly proclaimed that the creation of nineteen Israeli settlements on Palestinian prime agricultural land in the Gaza Strip was an evil deed that was decided upon and performed by Israeli politicians and people. They denounce it as an act of robbery, colonialism, and aggression.

Think of it, these Palestinian spokespersons demand: Several thousand Jewish settlers now own 35 percent of the land in the Gaza Strip and use it to enrich themselves. At the same time, 1.1 million Palestinians, many of them impoverished refugees and their progeny, reside on the rest of the land and have no economic opportunities. As an act committed during the Israeli military occupation of the Gaza Strip, the establishment of these nineteen Jewish settlements violates all international agreements and codes. No wonder, they add, that Israel's settlement policy has been repeatedly condemned by the United Nations and by many other international bodies.

Jewish members of the Israeli peace camp, which includes at least 20 percent of the Jewish population in Israel, agree with the Palestinians. They publicly denounce the argument of some of the settlers that they are ardent Zionists or that they are faithful Jews who are fulfilling their historical mission. It is indeed a fact that the confiscated areas of Palestinian land within the Gaza Strip, in which the Jewish settlements were set up, had nothing to do with the original goals of Zionism. Remember, Zionism was constituted as a movement which wanted to establish a homeland for the Jewish people by peaceful means. Nowhere in the history of Zionism, members of the Israeli peace camp continually remind their fellow Israelis, was there a decision that the return of the Jews to the land of Israel should be accompanied by robbery of the land from the indigenous Palestinians so as to enrich a few thousand Jews. Moreover, they add, there is enough land in the south of Israel, the Negev, for tens of thousands of Jewish settlers.

In denouncing the settlements in the Gaza Strip, members of the Peace Camp in Israel also rely on the Bible. They explain that the confiscated areas of land in the Gaza Strip do not have any link to the relationship of the Children of Israel to the land of Israel in Biblical times. The entire area of the Gaza Strip was never settled by the tribes of the Children of Israel, neither in Biblical times nor in the twenty-five centuries that followed. Thus, these peace-searching Israelis state, it is false to state that there are historical reasons for this Israeli state-inspired robbery of Palestinian land and state-inspired colonialism in the Gaza Strip.

It is also false, they proclaim, to suggest that there were so-called security reasons for establishing Jewish settlements in the Gaza Strip. The opposite is the case. Once they were established, these settlements became a severe security problem for the Israeli army. The seventeen families who reside in Netsarim, one of the Israeli settlements on the outskirts of Gaza City, need 800 Israeli soldiers to guard them daily and ensure their freedom of movement. An Israeli economist who belongs to the Peace Camp calculated that if the Israeli government were to pay to house each of the seventeen families in a suite of rooms in a first class hotel in Israel for a year, with all meals included, the cost would come to less than half of what the Israeli army currently spends each year to guard these settlers—who are enriching themselves by exploiting Palestinian labor on land robbed from the Palestinians.

Together with other members of the Israeli Peace Camp, we believe that Israeli greed, and greed alone, is the major reason for the confiscation of Palestinian land in the Gaza Strip and the handing of it to a few thousand Jews so that they can settle on it and enrich themselves. In an area as small, impoverished, and crowded as the Gaza Strip, these settlements, these embodiments of greed, stick out like a sore thumb. Other researchers of this topic might add a pinch of Israeli superciliousness and smugness to the pernicious greed that led to these wicked policies and deeds. Whatever the final list of ingredients that make up this witches' brew of political decisions and actions, we agree with what almost all world statesmen and many Israelis have announced: The Israeli settlements are a curse upon justice. They are also a bane to the daily life of many of the Palestinians in the Gaza Strip. Consequently, each of the Israeli settlers daily shares the responsibility for one of the prominent evils performed by the Israeli governments during Israel's ongoing military occupation of the Gaza Strip.

We will give only one additional example of the unfair political decisions that Israel has made during its three decades of military occupation of the Gaza Strip. This example has to do with the lack of drinking water and water for agriculture for the Palestinians residing in the Gaza Strip.

The water needs of the Gaza Strip are estimated to be 110 million cubes of water per year. Each year rainfall replenishes the Gaza Strip aquafer with approximately sixty million cubes of water. Thus, at least during the past quarter century, every year fifty million cubes of water are lacking in order to fulfill the basic water needs of this impoverished population. Israel is willing to sell the residents of the Gaza Strip the fifty million cubes of water that it lacks, but at a very high price.

Where does Israel get the water that it is willing to sell to the Palestinians in the Gaza Strip? We will not fully answer the question, yet we note one detail that is significant. Israel pumps at least 400 million cubes of water from the aquifer of the West Bank out of wells situated on Palestinian land. Israel sank these wells and pumps their water as a military occupier, without consulting the Palestinians who own the land and without paying them for their water. According to all human customs and laws, water pumped from Palestinian land belongs to the Palestinians. Israel acts otherwise. It uses the 400 million cubes of the water pumped from Palestinian land for its own consumption and is willing to sell the Palestinians in the Gaza Strip fifty million cubes of water at a very high price.

Let us repeat a few obvious facts. The Palestinians residing in the Gaza Strip and on the West Bank of the Jordan River are one nation. Hence the water that

Israel pumps out of the West Bank belongs to the Palestinian nation. Palestinian sources have repeatedly denounced Israel's policy of pumping 400 million cubes of Palestinian water out of the West Bank every year without paying the Palestinians for this water and then offering the Palestinians in the Gaza Strip, who lack potable water, fifty million cubes of water at high prices.

Because they lack the financial means to purchase Israeli water, the Palestinians in the Gaza Strip buy little water from the Israelis. Instead, they overpump their wells. As a result, the water in the Gaza Strip has become saline and highly tainted with poisonous minerals. Today, the tap water in most of the Gaza Strip is unfit for drinking; it will certainly cause the population long-term health problems. In stark contrast to this situation, the Israeli settlers in the Gaza Strip get their water directly from Israel at a subsidized price. They have built swimming pools, in which they delightedly bathe.

We can here terminate this brief overview, which provides some insight as to the bleak and oppressive situation created by Israeli military rule in the Gaza Strip. This overbearing situation was the background to the eruption of the Palestinian intifada in December 1987 and its continuation for six years.

Our overview also indicates why the Palestinians believe that during the intifada they were struggling for freedom, human dignity, human rights, and justice. Until now, however, we have only presented some external facts pertaining to this struggle. These external facts and other facts pertinent to the Israeli military rule will become much more vivid when seen through the lives and narratives of the six Palestinians whom we cite in Part 2.

NOTE

1. Sara Roy, *The Gaza Strip: The Political Economy of De-development* (Washington, DC: Institute for Palestine Studies, 1995).

Chapter 2

Rivca Gordon and Haim Gordon

Our personal involvement in the Gaza Strip began in February 1988, shortly after the intifada erupted in December 1987. When the intifada spread quickly and encompassed many people and groups at all levels of Palestinian society, we realized that we were witnessing a popular uprising of the Palestinian people who wished to live in freedom as an independent nation. What was occurring was definitely not a series of civil disruptions of the Israeli military rule, as Israeli government spokespersons attempted to portray the uprising. We grasped, as did many other Israelis, that the Palestinian people in the Gaza Strip and the West Bank were struggling for their political and personal freedom.

Israeli military rule of the Palestinian people in the Gaza Strip and the West Bank was not a new phenomenon. It had commenced after the June 1967 war, when Israeli armed forces occupied the West Bank, which had been part of the Kingdom of Jordan, and the Gaza Strip, which had been under Egyptian military rule. During that war, Israel had also occupied the Golan Heights, which belonged to Syria, and the Sinai Peninsula, which belonged to Egypt. But while the Golan Heights and the Sinai Peninsula had a very sparse population, the West Bank and the Gaza Strip were inhabited by close to a million and a half Palestinians.

As mentioned, in early 1988, we recognized that these Palestinians, whose population had grown to two million in the twenty-one years of Israeli military occupation, began a stone-throwing struggle so as to attain their freedom. We realized that the Palestinians who undertook this struggle wished to be recognized as an independent nation and to live on their land as a free people. In a word, they demanded that the Israelis terminate the military occupation of Palestinian land and the military rule of the Palestinian people.

With the eruption of the intifada, we faced an immediate problem. The oppressors were Israelis, like ourselves. Israeli soldiers who were suppressing the intifada were following orders that were given by Israeli politicians. But by fulfilling these orders, the Israeli soldiers were denying the freedom of the Palestinian people, who deserve to live in freedom, as do all human beings. They were forcefully oppressing two million Palestinians who wanted to live in freedom. This evil done by members of our nation enraged us. We wanted to fight it.

Philosophers have repeatedly stated that if you harshly destroy another person's freedom, you are doing evil. Some philosophers add that in the process, you are also ruining your own existence. We decided that our responsibility, as Israelis, was to utilize democratic means in order to fight the evil that was being done by the Israeli armed forces to the Palestinian people. We knew that the Israeli armed forces were fulfilling political goals of the Israeli government; hence, our struggle was also against Israeli government decisions and policies. But to initiate such a struggle against our own army and our own government, we had to learn in much greater detail what was happening in the Occupied Territories. We also had to choose a direction for our struggle.

It seemed quite natural for us to learn what was happening by visiting the Gaza Strip, which was less than fifty kilometers from Beer Sheva, where we reside. In early 1988, the Gaza Strip was home to about 860,000 Palestinians. Around 75 percent of the Palestinians residing in the Gaza Strip were refugees and their progeny; all the refugees had fled from their land in southern Palestine during Israel's 1948 War of Independence. In early 1988, together with other Israelis from Beer Sheva, we established the Gaza Team for Human Rights, whose stated mission was to engage in democratic activities that would help protect the human rights of the Palestinians in the Gaza Strip. We are the only founding members of the Gaza Team who are still active in the Gaza Strip. Over the past fourteen years, quite a few dedicated and concerned Israelis have joined the Gaza Team. All of them left the team after a period of hard work; at times this period lasted a few years. As members of the Gaza Team, they shared in our work and frequently enlightened us.

One of the first decisions of the Gaza Team was that we would not be so-called social workers. We refused to limit our activities to helping those Palestinians who suffered from the Israeli occupation. We recognized that helping people who are downtrodden and oppressed can lighten their burden and may enhance their existence. Still, we believed that fighting for freedom requires more than helping people who are suffering under military rule. Struggling for freedom means fighting against the oppressors. In addition, we firmly believed that we were struggling for a State of Israel that pursues justice in its relations with its neighbors.

We chose to fight for the human rights of the Palestinian people which was denied them by the Israeli military rule. During the past fourteen years, that struggle has determined our orientation towards what is happening in Israel and the Occupied Territories. It dictated the language that we used; it determined the approaches that we adopted to support the Palestinian quest and fight for freedom. It also influenced our decision to work on this book together with Taher Shriteh.

In a nutshell, we grasped that our decision to fight meant that we must seek democratic ways to confront and reject those Israeli politicians and simple people who, utilizing the force of the Israeli army and military establishment, were forcefully denying the Palestinian people their basic right to live in freedom.

Someone may say: Your description concerning Israeli evil is still not clear. Give an example of evil that you confronted and fought. What did you do in the Gaza Strip? How did you fight what you call Israeli evil by democratic means?

After a few months of learning the situation in the Gaza Strip, we decided to struggle by bringing to light complaints by Palestinians concerning the abuse of their human rights by Israeli soldiers. Five or six members of the Gaza Team would travel to the Gaza Strip once every two to three weeks for a full day. There we met Palestinians whose human rights had been trampled upon and abused by soldiers in the Israeli army; we carefully recorded each individual complaint and sent all the complaints to the Israeli military authorities. The recipient of the majority of our complaints was General Matan Vilnai, the commander of the Southern Command of the Israeli army, which includes the Gaza Strip. We sent copies of some of the complaints to Israeli civil authorites. To each complaint we added the statement: If the complaint proves to be factually true, the following is our evaluation of the incident. We gave our evaluation and demanded a responsible answer.

Two Palestinians from Gaza City who helped us gather complaints from their fellow Palestinians were the lawyer Freh Abu-Medin, who later became minister of justice of the Palestinian Authority, and the businessman Awni El Hasham. Both of them gave us full access to their offices and invited any Palestinian whose human rights had been abused by Israeli soldiers to come to their offices in order to meet us. Often we would encounter a dozen Palestinians waiting for us when we came to one of their offices. Many other Palestinians also helped us in simple tasks such as translating complaints or bringing us to areas where human rights abuses had been performed.

The exigencies of the situation dictated where in the Gaza Strip we would gather the complaints. Quite often we would visit the homes of Palestinians in rural areas and in the refugee camps of the Gaza Strip, where people had been brutally harmed by Israeli soldiers. There we could hear their complaints on the spot.

Here are two severe complaints concerning abuse of human rights out of hundreds of complaints by Palestinians that we recorded and sent to the Israeli military authorities during the intifada. In our letter that accompanied each of the following complaints we noted that if the complaint was true, then what had been done was evil, unlawful, and brought shame on Israel and its army. We demanded an immediate inquiry and we requested a detailed response.

Complaint by Nezam Muhammad Abu-Daka, Identification Number: 963521075, from Khan Yunis, concerning brutal torture by Israeli security service officers.

"On July 10, 1990, I returned to Israel from my studies in Libya through the Jordan Bridge. After I crossed the bridge, I was immediately arrested. I was accused of belonging to an organization linked to the intifada and of receiving army training in Libya. I denied the charges. Despite these denials, I spent sixty days in Israeli prisons. I was transferred from prison to prison four times. Each time I was forced to lie face down and handcuffed on the back of a truck with the Israeli soldiers beating me on my back and neck all the way.

"Here are some of the tortures I went through. In Kfar Yona Prison every morning two men came into my cell and immediately began beating me while I lay on the floor with my hands and feet tied. They beat the soles of my feet and the back of my neck, and they stood on my stomach. I got nothing to drink. When I couldn't bear the thirst anymore, I forced myself to drink the toilet water. In Gaza Central Prison, I was tortured from Sunday until Friday and not allowed to sleep. The interrogator's name was Abu-Zaim. He told me: 'You were put among collaborators and they didn't make you speak. Now we'll help you to tell us everything.' He referred to my stay in Nablus Prison, where I was put in a room with forty collaborators. They tried to convince me to disclose all my deeds in Libya to them, in order—thus they argued—that they could convey this information to their Palestinian leaders. I told them nothing. Nor did I say anything to the interrogator, simply because I was not ready to confess something that I hadn't done. In response to my silence, I was thrown into a small cell called the refrigerator, which is constantly kept at freezing temperatures. The cold was unbearable, especially since I was in there for about ten hours. Worse was the fact that I was not allowed to go to the toilet and had to relieve myself on the floor. Since the cell was tiny, I later had to sit on my excrement.

"Two interrogators in Gaza Central Prison who tortured me were Steve and Jack; they used my body as an object for karate training. They would tie my hands and feet to rings in the wall; then, on my body, Jack taught Steve the warring principles of karate. These training exercises continued every day for thirty-five days, twice during the morning and twice at night. At times I was not tied to the wall, but my hands were tied behind my back. Jack would then hold my shoulders from behind, while kicking me and hitting my head on the wall. Then he would show Steve how to do the same thing. Or Jack would hit me under my chest with a karate blow and show Steve how to hit me so that it would hurt, yet would not leave a trace. While Steve was hitting me, Jack instructed him as to how to do it precisely and in accordance with karate principles. For weeks, each day I was, for hours, a live puppet for their karate training. I want to stress this point. These beatings went on for hours, often without them asking me one question. Yet they called it interrogation.

"Another interrogator, Benny, used a different manner of torture. He tied my hands behind my back, took out a pack of cigarettes without filters, filled my mouth with cigarettes, and lit them. Holding a club, he told me that I must smoke all the cigarettes that were in my mouth at once. No cigarette was to fall until it burned my lips. If a cigarette fell before I finished it, he put it back in my mouth. When a cigarette was finished and burned my lips, he immediately replaced it with a new cigarette. If I dared to spit a cigarette out, he immediately hit me on the head, murderously, with the club. He continued with this torture until I finished smoking the whole pack. His goal was to fill my lungs with smoke so that I would faint, which often happened. He never asked me a question. Sadism alone motivated him.

"I was released after sixty days in prison. No charge was brought against me. I was tortured for nothing. The interrogators' sole goal was to inflict suffering upon me."[1]

The second complaint has to do with the killing of an Israeli soldier in El Bureij Refugee Camp by an incensed mob of Palestinians in September 1990. The Israeli soldier had entered the camp alone and by mistake, and was gang-murdered. We, of course, firmly condemn such evil deeds as gang-murder. Yet we also condemn the Israeli response. Here is one of the complaints that we received and sent to General Matan Vilnai, that describes the actions of Israeli soldiers and officers of the security service after the brutal murder of the Israeli soldier.

Complaint concerning beatings, cruelty, and sexual abuse filed by Fatma Atta Abdel Jawad Azahra, Identification Number: 958976763, from El Bureij Refugee Camp.

"On Thursday, September 20, 1990, at 11:00 P.M., an Israeli army officer and twenty soldiers from a Givati army unit forcefully entered my house. They searched the house, messing up everything. They asked: 'Where are the men?' They were seeking my fifteen-year-old son, Rami, and my husband. I explained that they both went in the morning to Gaza City to bring goods for our store, that they were not here when the killing of the Israeli soldier occurred, and that they could not return because of the curfew. The soldiers left. At midnight, they came to search again with Abu-Razal, a security service (Shabak) officer. The search was violent, but again they found nothing and left.

"The following night after midnight, when we were all asleep, Israeli paratroopers burst into our home after breaking down the door. With them was Abu-Rami, a Shabak officer who spoke Arabic. They searched everywhere. Following Abu-Rami's orders, they broke doors, furniture, kitchen utensils. Again I was asked about my husband and my son. I replied that my husband and son had not returned, probably because of the curfew that was still being enforced in our camp. They asked about our other children and I replied that they were asleep upstairs. Abu Rami went up. He picked up every child, five girls and four boys, and threw each one down the stairs. The soldiers pushed all the children, together with their seventy-year-old grandfather, into a room, locked the door, and a soldier put the key into his pocket. Abu-Rami told me to come with him upstairs. Suddenly, he saw a child still sleeping. Abu-Rami ordered a soldier to take the child downstairs and put him with the other childen. The soldier grabbed the boy by his neck and, while strangling him, dragged him downstairs. He then put him, half-conscious, with the other children. Abu-Rami told me to bring my husband and Rami. I insisted that I didn't know where they were. He beat me with his hands and gun on my body, face, and breasts. He threatened, 'If you don't bring your husband and son, your children will remain alone and you, you'll be thrown among the soldiers and they'll fuck you as much as they want.'

"I was so frightened by these threats that I told Abu-Rami that perhaps my husband and my son were at my parents' house in Nuseirat Refugee Camp. He told me to take him there. I said, 'I can't come alone with you. I'm a woman. Let me take one of my babies with me.' He refused, grabbed me by the shoulder, and dragged me outside. He told a soldier to bring my sister-in-law, Mirvat, who is my neighbor. Mirvat was brought and stood with her arms folded. Abu-Rami hit her and said, 'When you stand in front of a Shabak officer, don't you dare fold your arms.'

"Mirvat and I were put in an army jeep and driven under guard to Nuseirat Refugee Camp. On the way the soldiers who were guarding us beat me and cursed me. They repeatedly said, 'You're not beautiful, and we'll take you to the soldiers and they'll fuck you.' Then they added, 'Our daughters are more beautiful than yours.' We arrived at my parents' house in Nuseirat Refugee Camp around 5:00 A.M. The soldiers left Mirvat and me outside under guard and burst into my parents' house. My husband and son were not there. Later I learned that all my family members had been beaten."

During the fall of 1990, we sent both of the above cited complaints to General Matan Vilnai and to the office of the general prosecutor in Israel. We never received a reply, even though both complaints were published in the Israeli newspaper *Hadoshot*, to which we sent these and similar complaints. The army spokesperson told the reporter of *Hadoshot* that it would examine the complaints and soon present a full response. No such response was ever presented. Since both the Gaza Team and *Hadoshot* received no response to the above complaints, we can say that the incidents and the facts described in the complaints were never denied. Given this lack of denial, and also on the basis of our lengthy experience struggling for human rights in the Gaza Strip, we believe the complaints to be true.

Our years of gathering complaints concerning the abuse of human rights taught us that when a Palestinian agreed to lodge a formal complaint against the Israeli authorities and gave us his or her identification number and full name, that Palestinian felt that he or she was endangering oneself. Israeli military authorities might respond, the Palestinian thought, by finding a way to punish him or her. That may be a major reason that we believe that more than 99 percent of the complaints that we filed were true. In a situation of military occupation, we assume that few simple people would endanger themselves so as to spread a lie.

Hold it! someone may say. You mentioned that you sent many complaints to the Israeli authorities. Was the official response to all your complaints similar to what you already described?

In order to answer this question, we wish to give an additional, quite detailed example of our struggle against the abuses of Palestinian human rights by the Israeli military and civilian authorities in the Gaza Strip. This example has to do with our struggle against the minister of defense and the office of the Israeli general prosecutor.

During the first six years of its activities, the Gaza Team for Human Rights sent approximately one thousand complaints to Israeli authorities. The complaints described instances of violations of Palestinian human rights by the soldiers in the Israel Defense Force. Many of these complaints were not answered; other complaints did not receive the attention that they deserved; still others were answered in a manner that members of the Gaza Team believed to be grossly irresponsible or false. We decided to act and to demand a responsible answer to those complaints that had been ignored. In this struggle we pretty much failed, but the story of the failure is instructive and significant.

A few months after the signing of the Oslo Peace Agreement between Yitzchak Rabin and Yasser Arafat, the Gaza Team sent the following letter to Prime Minister Rabin. To the letter were attached 129 complaints that were similar to the two complaints cited above and had been sent to Israeli authorities between 1990 and 1994; we had received no response to these 129 complaints.

Here is the letter.

January 16, 1994

Mr. Rabin
Prime Minister and Defense Minister

Mr. Rabin Shalom,

I am writing to you as chairwoman of the Gaza Team. Since the beginning of the intifada, the Gaza Team has been working to ensure the human rights of the Palestinians in the Gaza Strip. We have filed hundreds of complaints about abuses of human rights by Israeli forces. Except in a few cases, the complaints were always sent to General Matan Vilnai, who is in charge of the Southern Command. We assumed that since General Vilnai is the senior officer in the area, he is therefore responsible for everything that occurs, including the ensuring of human rights of the Palestinians.

Lately I went over the complaints sent to General Vilnai since 1990. What became evident was the negligence of the army in relation to many of the complaints sent by the Gaza Team. In many cases the Israel Defense Force (IDF) did not respond or did not confirm receiving the complaint. When it did confirm receiving the complaint and notified us that an investigation had been initiated, it did not convey to us the results of the investigation, although it had promised to do so. We were also frequently notified that the files containing specific complaints had been closed because, the IDF held, the witnesses did not appear to testify.

I protest against the existence of a category of complaints whereby the IDF closes the file because the person complaining did not show up to be investigated after being requested to come. Such a response is evasive, to say the least, for the following reasons. First, if, according to the complaint, there is a suspicion that Israeli soldiers did not act in accordance with the rules and the orders that they received, the case should be fully and wholeheartedly investigated! Second, the IDF is very capable of finding Palestinians when it is seeking for them. The fact that precisely in those cases when there are complaints against soldiers of the IDF, the IDF is incapable of finding those Palestinians who complained constitutes an evasion of public responsibility. When such a phenomenon is repeated systematically, one begins to doubt the wish of the commander in charge to examine the responsibility of the soldiers for blatant abuses of human rights. And, third, some of the complaints rouse the suspicion that there were criminal acts. (See, for instance, complaint no. 63.) The unwillingness of the IDF to do everything in order to reach the Palestinians who complained can be considered a support of criminal acts, or an attempt to sweep them under the rug. In any event such a closing of files does not bring honor to the IDF.

I would like to point out that most of the following complaints—126 out of 129—were sent to General Matan Vilnai. There were cases in which copies were sent to other government bodies. They responded pretty much in the same manner as the IDF. I would like to emphasize that I sent between 1–5 reminders to every complaint to which General Vilnai decided not to respond. In most cases I received no answer to the reminders from General Vilnai.

I will present most of the complaints briefly. It is possible that some of the complaints did not reach General Vilnai's office; it is also possible that some of the responses sent by General Vilnai did not reach me. In any event, such is a minority of the cases. They cannot change the serious fact that General Vilnai is not fulfilling his responsibility as senior officer of the area in relation to the human rights of the Palestinians living in the Gaza Strip.

The 129 complaints attached to this letter reveal that primarily General Matan Vilnai, but also Dorit Banish [the Public Prosecutor] and the commander of the border police were negligent in treating the problems of abuse of human rights that were addressed to them. We are therefore requesting you to do the following:

1. Notify those responsible to give answers to the attached complaints do so immediately.

2. Appoint a person who will investigate why there was such negligence. The investigator should reach conclusions regarding those who acted negligently.

In passing we would like to mention that any attempt to appoint Mr. Haim Yisraeli as the investigator will be seen by us as an evasion. Mr. Yisraeli has written us several letters that included lies. See, for instance, complaint no. 1.

During the last six months General Vilnai has developed a method whereby he refers the Gaza Team to other government bodies. Thus, the murdering of a Palestinian child in the Gaza Strip is not a matter that concerns General Vilnai if the suspected murderer is from the border police. Also, what is termed in the attached documents the "Rafah Massacre" is not a matter for which the senior commander of the Gaza Strip feels that he is responsible. It seems that General Vilnai believes that if members of the border police massacre Palestinians in the Shabura Refugee Camp it is a private matter for the commander of the border police and that he, General Vilnai, has no responsibility for what has occurred. We see such behavior as an attempt not to allow the residents of the Gaza Strip to receive the help they deserve when their legitimate rights are offended. It is also a cynical approach, bordering on evil, on the part of General Vilnai. It is not necessary to add that by adopting such an approach General Vilnai is not fulfilling his responsibility towards the Israeli nation. Nor is his behavior honorable to the IDF.

Every person who complained to us gave his ID number and his full name, trusting that the IDF is interested in relating sincerely to his complaint. By doing so all of these Palestinians also expressed the expectations of the majority of the Israeli population—that the IDF will act honorably while respecting the human rights of any and every person.

The fact that so many Palestinians turned to us for help already testifies to the fact that it is very difficult for Palestinians to receive help from the occupying administration of the IDF. Furthermore, when General Vilnai also ignores the complaints of Israeli citizens who are trying to help the IDF to act honorably, his negligence and his attempts to flee from responsibility by bureaucratic measures ruin the trust of Israelis and Palestinians in the IDF. The scorn with which so many reporters and journalists relate to the saying "the IDF is investigating" is a result, among other things, of the negligence that screams from the attached complaints, and from the scorning of Palestinian human rights by General Matan Vilnai.

I am sending a copy of this letter and the attached complaints to a few Knesset members, to the press, and to the lawyers who help the Gaza Team ensure the human rights of the Palestinians.

I would appreciate receiving confirmation that this letter arrived in your office, and also that you notify me what you plan to do concerning our above requests.

Sincerely,

Rivca Gordon

Chairwoman, Gaza Team

Yitzchak Rabin never answered the above letter. His office acknowledged receipt of the letter and notified us that a detailed answer would be forthcoming from the chief army legal officer. Such an answer never arrived. After waiting five months and sending reminders to the chief army legal officer and to Mr. Rabin, the Gaza Team appealed to the High Court of Justice. (The High Court of Justice is a special sitting of at least three supreme court justices who deal with an appeal which argues that in a specific case a branch of the government is acting unjustly.) The Gaza Team appealed that the government be instructed to give a specific, detailed, relevant answer to each of the 129 complaints.

The army and the general prosecutor's office seemed to fear having to face the High Court of Justice. A few days before the scheduled hearing in April 1995, Shai Nitzan, a senior lawyer in the general prosecutor's office, sent our lawyer answers to the 129 complaints, forcing us to cancel our appeal.

We studied the government answers carefully. Here are some examples of our complaints and the answers that we received from Shai Nitzan. These examples will help to support our conclusions.

Complaint #106: On May 12, 1993 we sent a letter to General Matan Vilnai which included a complaint by Mustafa Halil Ibrahim concerning the killing of thirteen-year-old Mahmad Taima of refugee camp Shabura on that day by Israeli soldiers. Mustafa saw what happened. Not far from where Mustafa stood was a house with an Israeli army lookout post, with twelve Israeli soldiers around it. A hundred meters from the house a few five- and six-year-old children threw stones in the direction of the soldiers. Mahmad Taima was walking alone about fifty meters from these soldiers. Suddenly one shot was fired, probably by one of the soldiers near the house. Taima fell with a bullet in his stomach. He died in the hospital. On May 24, 1993 the IDF notified us that an investigation had been launched and results would be forthcoming. To date, we have received no report on the results of the investigation.

Response of Shai Nizan to complaint #106: An investigation was launched after receipt of the complaint in file: 115/93 Gaza. On June 11, 1994 the prosecutor's office decided to close the file without taking steps against anyone.

Complaint #88: On August 23, 1992, we sent the complaint of Isa Mahmud Abu Arifa from refugee camp Shabura to General Matan Vilnai. The complaint dealt with the sufferings of Isa Mahmud's son Raed, who from June 1991 to August 1992 was repeatedly subject to violent arrests, torture, and attacks by Israeli soldiers. One time Raed was caught by Israeli soldiers, forced into a jeep, and beaten with clubs all over his body; he suffered a brain concussion. He was released without being charged. Another time Raed was arrested and taken to a police station for interrogation. He was beaten until he fainted and was taken to the army doctor. The army doctor said Raed had suffered from a fit of epilepsy and gave him medicine. Again he was released without being charged. One night soldiers forcefully entered the house looking for Raed and stole money and jewelry. They went to seek Raed in the house of his brother, Iyad, and beat Iyad until he lost consciousness. They also beat and cursed Iyad's wife. After the Israeli soldiers left, Iyad was taken to a hospital where he lay ill for some days. Iyad was never charged.

This complaint was also sent to the general prosecutor's office and to the Israeli chief of police. On September 3, 1992, the IDF announced that the complaint had been passed on to the appropriate authorities. On September 7, 1992, the chief of police affirmed receipt of the complaint. No additional answer was received.

Response of Shai Nitzan to complaint #88: The complaint was transferred to the police force. Therefore, it is suggested to write on the matter to the ministry of police. (Note that we sent the complaint to the Israeli authorities in 1992, and Shai Nitzan was writing in 1995.)

Complaints #26 and #27: On April 22, 1993, we sent a letter to General Matan Vilnai with the complaint of Samir Mahmud Ahmed Abu-Daka from Abasan. On May 5, 1993, we sent a letter to General Matan Vilnai with the complaint of Mahmad Nafa Salam Abu-Daka from Abasan. Both complaints describe Israeli soldiers forcing Palestinians to break open and unearth graves in the Pirhan graveyard. The soldiers were allegedly seeking hidden arms deposited in the graves. Mahmad Nafa noted that an Israeli officer from the civil administration arrived later and apologized for the deed. Both Samir Mahmud and Mahmad Nafa demand a full investigation and punishment of those involved in this sacrilegious deed. (The Gaza Team photographed the opened graves.)

Response of Shai Nitzan to complaints #26 & #27: The complaints were investigated, file #138/93. No evidence was found in support of the complaints, and no soldiers were traced who could be questioned as suspects who instigated a search in the graveyard.

We wish to briefly analyze the government answers to the blatant abuses of human rights performed by Israeli soldiers in the Gaza Strip that were described in the complaints. First, however, it is important to again emphasize a major reason for Shai Nitzan's evasive answers. Six years of filing complaints concerning the abuse of human rights taught the Gaza Team that, when responding to complaints, in almost all cases the IDf investigators do not investigate Palestinians. Both Samir Mahmud and Mahmad Nafa, who filed complaints about the unearthing of graves, were never called to give testimony. Nor was Mustafa Halil Ibrahim called to testify about the killing of Mahmad Taima. As mentioned in Rivca Gordon's letter to Prime Minister Rabin, the fact that IDF investigators reach conclusions without ever hearing those who complained was checked by the Gaza Team in dozens of cases, including the above cited cases. This fact is known to the general prosecutor's office and to Shai Nitzan. Since Palestinians who filed complaints were almost never called to testify, it is clear that the persons conducting the investigations rarely—if ever—did what was needed to get to the truth of a matter.

This skewed investigation creates a situation whereby the general prosecutor's office cannot relate to facts. Note that Shai Nitzan never denies the evidence of the above complaints. In response to complaint #106 he doesn't deny that Mahmad Taima died on May 12, 1993, as a result of a bullet shot by Israeli soldiers. He doesn't deny that thirteen-year-old Mahmad Taima was no threat to the Israeli soldiers who shot him. He doesn't cast doubts on the testimony of Mustafa Halil Ibrahim.

Shai Nitzan doesn't deny any of the facts related to the unwarranted beatings of Raed and his family or the robbery of their jewels and money by IDF soldiers. He referred us to the ministry of the police who notified us that the officer in charge denied the complaint, hence the file was closed. As in most cases, the Palestinians involved were never called to testify.

In relation to the breaking open of graves, Shai Nitzan is much more clever. He doesn't deny the facts or the testimonies of two people. He says that no evidence was found by IDF investigators. Shai Nitzan does not wonder how evidence can be found if the investigators never visited the graveyard, which is what we were told by Palestinians; nor does he note that the people who complained were never called to testify. What Shai Nitzan's answer means is that a few Israeli soldiers were asked if they knew about the unearthing of graves, and they all answered that they had never heard of such an event. The same is true of almost all 94 out of the 129 complaints which deal with unwarranted violent abuse of Palestinians by Israeli soldiers. The violence included beatings, killings, and destruction of property. Shai Nitzan never challenged the facts; in a few cases, like the case of the unearthed graves, he writes that he didn't find evidence.

Thus, the answers of Shai Nitzan and the general prosecutor's office reveal no effort to get to the truth. Their responses to the complaints of the Gaza Team are merely a constructed cover-up for the army, so that it will not be shamed in the High Court of Justice. That explains why Shai Nitzan responded in the manner of a second-rate bureaucrat who is merely shuffling papers so as not to assume responsibility.

In a few cases, the IDF notified the Gaza Team that Palestinians had been called three times to testify and had not appeared, hence the file had been closed. In three cases that we checked, the Palestinians denied ever being called to testify. Yet, in the above letter Rivca Gordon also notified the IDF that it is their responsibility to find the Palestinian who made the complaint and ask him or her to testify. Here is Shai Nitzan's answer to that argument in complaint #63: "The fact that someone complained and presents certain arguments, but is unwilling to come to testify, is not a reason to *endanger* an investigator by sending him to the house of the Palestinian so that he may agree to complain. The law in the State of Israel and in other places is that whoever wishes to complain presents oneself at the police station." (Emphasis in original.)

Shai Nitzan seems never to have noticed the dozens of instances documented in the Israeli press in which Palestinians who complained to the authorities about behavior of Israeli soldiers were beaten or humiliated by the Israeli police or the Israeli army authorities to whom they turned for help. When the Gaza Team suggested to some Palestinians that they complain to the authorities, most Palestinians thought we were either joking or did not know that we were sending them to be punished. Complaining to the Israeli authorities, they told us, meant entering an Israeli army base where Palestinians were often humiliated and at times beaten or even jailed. Who needs such an experience?

Much more important is the due process of justice which Shai Nitzan and the general prosecutor's office ignore. Due process requires that when a supposed murder occurs, as in the case of thirteen-year-old Mahmad Taima, the responsibility of the authorities is to find any shred of evidence so as to discover the truth of the matter. Who killed Mahmad Taima? Why? Not questioning a person who saw what happened is an evasion of due process and a humiliation of justice. When seeking witnesses to a supposed murder in Israel, the police do not wait for witnesses to come to them; they seek them out. The Israeli bullet in the body of Mahmad Taima is sufficient for an investigation to be launched and every possible witness to be diligently sought. That did not happen in this case nor in dozens of similar cases of our reports of killings, beatings, or robbery by Israeli soldiers. Shai Nitzan is merely presenting an argument that will justify the Israeli army's cover-up.

One more point that Rivca Gordon makes in her letter is worth repeating. When Israeli authorities wanted to question a Palestinian on any other topic besides the human rights abuses of the Israeli soldiers, they almost always found the Palestinian.

We wish to present a numerical breakdown of the 129 complaints and the responses that we received from Shai Nitzan. Ninety-four of the 129 complaints had to do with violent abuses. The remaining thirty-five were complaints of Palestinians who were not allowed to travel abroad, or were not allowed family reunions, or suffered other manners of bureaucratic harassment. In his response of April 1995, Shai Nitzan argued that the travel and family reunion complaints were now irrelevant, since the Gaza Strip is now under Palestinian rule. He also held that some of the complainants had received an answer directly, which was not always true. He did not refer to the fact, central to our appeal, that some Palestinians had to wait two years or more for an answer.

Here is a breakdown of the ninety-four complaints of violent abuses and the answers that the Gaza Team received. Some of the complaints included more than one instance of violent abuse; for instance, deliberate property damage often occurred together with violent beatings. Complaint #88, cited above, includes beatings and robbery. We will indicate when the Gaza Team received nonevasive answers, what the answers were, and the number of such nonevasive answers. We wish to stress again that the facts presented in our complaints were never challenged.

1. Eighteen complaints related to Palestinians killed by Israeli soldiers. All complaints had to do with cases where there was no threat to the soldiers. Five of the Palestinians killed were children under the age of fourteen; one was a man eighty-five years old. In only one case was an Israeli officer put on trial for negligence. All other answers were evasive, similar to the answers presented above.

2. Ten complaints related to sexual harassment by Israeli soldiers or members of the security service. In one case a soldier was put on trial for inappropriate behavior. All other answers were evasive.

3. Forty-two complaints related to beatings and gross humiliation of Palestinians. All answers were evasive.

4. Thirty-four complaints related to unwarranted destruction of property. In four cases, Shai Nitzan notified us that Palestinians had received compensation for the destroyed property. All other answers were evasive.

5. Seven complaints were of money or jewelry stolen by Israeli soldiers during a house search. All answers were evasive.

6. Four complaints were of torture during incarceration. All answers were evasive.

Thus, the ninety-four complaints described 115 instances of violent abuses of Palestinian human rights by Israeli soldiers. No facts were denied. Only in relation to six instances of such abuse did the army have a reasonable answer. All other answers were evasive.

Our appeal to the High Court of Justice and the official Israeli response allowed us to draw broad conclusions, which we published. Here are some of those conclusions.

The Israeli government and army ignored the hundreds of complaints of abuse of Palestinian human rights by Israeli soldiers that were submitted by the Gaza Team and by other Israeli organizations that struggled for justice. The prime ministers of Israel and their subordinates supported the lack of response to these complaints by Israeli authorities. Thus, the argument that Israel did its utmost to respect the human rights of Palestinians during the occupation is false. Also false is the statement that violations of human rights occurred only in exceptional cases.

The truth of the matter is that gross violations of human rights were an everyday occurrence, countenanced by army officers and often initiated by officers of the security service. These violations were systematically covered up by all relevant government offices, including the office of the general prosecutor of Israel.

The above examples and our brief discussion provide some insight into the continual abuse of human rights in the Gaza Strip during the first seven years of our work, 1988–1995. Remember, we met with a very small segment of the population of the Gaza Strip. Yet the Gaza Team filed more than one thousand complaints about specific abuses of human rights of Palestinians by Israeli soldiers and military personnel. Many of the complaints were similar to those cited above. This vast number of filed complaints speaks for itself as to the evil done by the Israeli military forces to the Palestinians living in the Gaza Strip. No less significant is our finding that the facts of the more than thousand complaints that we sent were hardly ever denied.

We should mention that there were Israeli army officers on active duty who supported our work. These were mainly officers from the army unit that was called the Civil Administration, whose stated goal was to assist the Palestinian population in their everyday life under Israeli military rule. The officers of the Civil Administration wanted Israeli soldiers to act in accordance with military rules. Hence, whenever we reported instances in which soldiers blatantly breached military rules, the officers of the Civil Administration were willing to support our complaints. They also helped, at times, when a Palestinian was unable to cope with the Israeli military bureaucracy. Their assistance, however, was quite meager in the face of the onslaught of Israeli oppression.

In 1994, with the beginning of the implementation of what was called the Oslo Peace Process, the Gaza Strip was handed over to the Palestinian Authority. Israeli settlements in the Gaza Strip were not handed over; the settlements remained as enclaves inside Palestinian land and were considered to be part of Israel. This status was to be continued during an interim period until a final settlement was reached between Israel and the Palestinian Authority about how the neighboring nations would end the hostilities and live in good faith as neighbors. May 13, 1999, was announced by the parties involved in the negotiations to be the target date for terminating the interim period and reaching a final settlement. In the interim period, a joint force of Palestinian and Israeli soldiers was established to ensure the security of the Israeli settlers.

On paper, this agreement looked pretty good. But from the beginning, there were many Israelis and some Palestinians who did their utmost to make sure that the agreement failed. Looking back today we can say that the most significant deed that ensured the failure of the Israeli-Palestinian agreement was the assassination of Israeli Prime Minister Yitzchak Rabin by a Jewish right-wing fanatic. Since Rabin's death, no Israeli politician has had the vision, the fortitude, and the courage to terminate the Israeli occupation of Palestinian land and bring about a just and honorable peace with the Palestinians.

Two important developments in 1995 and 1996 somewhat changed the character of the work of the Gaza Team. Both developments, we believe, were linked to the attempts of many Israeli politicians and many high officers in the Israeli army to scuttle the so-called peace process. The first development was an unpublished decision by Israeli politicians and the Israeli military authorities to attempt to limit interaction between Israelis and Palestinians. The second development was an Israeli decision to attempt to limit the work of Israeli human rights groups working in the Gaza Strip. How were these decisions implemented?

One of the first acts of the Israeli military after Israel transferred the control of the Gaza Strip to the Palestinian Authority was to declare the entire Gaza Strip a "closed military zone." They stated that this declaration was for so-called security reasons. As a result of this declaration, Jewish Israelis were not allowed to enter the Gaza Strip without explicit permission from the Israeli army. Note that during our seven years of work during the intifada as the Gaza Team, from 1988 until 1995, we never had to ask permission in order to enter the Gaza Strip. Note also that the Israeli settlements in the Gaza Strip were not part of the "closed military zone," and Israelis did not need permission to visit the settlements.

Despite its being a closed military zone, Arab citizens of Israel were allowed to enter the Gaza Strip whenever they wished. In contrast, Jewish Israelis were permitted to enter the closed military zone of the Gaza Strip only if they had what the army considered to be a legitimate reason for entering the zone. In order to prove this legitimate reason, an Israeli had to have a formal invitation that had been issued by a recognized Palestinian organization in the Gaza Strip, saying that the organization invited the Jewish Israeli to visit them on a specific day. In the formal invitation, the Palestinian organization was also required to state that it would provide Palestinian guards who would ensure the security of the visiting Jewish Israeli.

We will not list the additional bureaucratic hurdles, thought up by the Israeli military authorities, which made entering and visiting the Gaza Strip extremely difficult for any Jewish Israeli. What is evident is that Israeli politicians and the Israeli military authorities did their utmost to limit interaction between Jewish Israelis and the Palestinians living in the Gaza Strip. Note again that all the decrees which strove to limit this interaction between Israeli Jews and Palestinians were enforced after Israel began implementing the Oslo Peace Agreement.

The Israeli authorities tried to limit the activities of human rights organizations in the Gaza Strip by announcing that the Palestinians residing in areas where the Palestinian Authority had assumed control did not need any other representation in order to protect their human rights. They stressed that the Palestinian Authority represented all the Palestinians, including those whose human rights were abused. Consequently, the Israelis argued, there was no need for the so-called interference of any other human rights advocates and nongovernment organizations. All that was needed, they stated, was for representatives of the Palestinian Authority to complain, and the complaints would be handled efficiently and in good faith.

From our broad experience, we can firmly state that this last statement was false. It concealed many abuses of human rights that Israelis continued to perform, as Palestinians at all levels of political influence repeatedly told us. Our appendix, which describes the plight of the fishermen in the Gaza Strip, shows in painful detail one example of the continual abuse of the human rights of Palestinians. The appendix also reveals the deceit of the Israeli military who stated that they always responded to Palestinian complaints about the abuse of human rights.

Israeli newspaper reporters and Palestinian officials repeatedly stated that Israeli military authorities usually scorned and ignored complaints and appeals by Palestinians concerning the abuse of their human rights, including those appeals transferred to them through the Palestinian Authority. We have no doubt, from our own experience with these Israeli military authorities, that the Israeli reporters and the Palestinian officials who related instances of scorn on the part of Israeli military establishment were telling the truth. Again, the appendix concerning the fishermen in the Gaza Strip reveals the cynicism and indifference of the Israeli military authorities in relation to the human rights of the Palestinians in the Gaza Strip. We are confident that the Israeli military authorities merely used the above argument about the Palestinian Authority representing all Palestinians to try to smother all activities by Israeli human rights organizations in the Gaza Strip.

The Gaza Team struggled firmly against both the decision to limit interaction between Israelis and Palestinians and the decision that all reports of Israeli human rights abuses should be filed by the Palestinian Authority. We enlisted a dozen Israeli Knesset members to support our struggles. Until the eruption of the second intifada, we regularly brought groups of Israelis to the Gaza Strip to teach them about the oppressive situation there, which is a direct result of Israeli military rule. As the appendix shows, we also continued to file complaints against the abuse of human rights of Palestinians.

NOTE

1. Testimony used by permission of Nezam Muhammad Abu-Daka.

Part 2

Narratives of Freedom Fighters

Chapter 3

Tahani Abu Daqa

I was born in July 1960, in Abasan in the Gaza Strip. I have an older brother, Ziad, and three younger sisters, and a very young brother. I had another sister, but she passed away recently. My young brother was born eighteen years after his older brother and brought great happiness to my mother, who wanted more than one male child. Most of my life, since my early childhood, my father did not live in the Gaza Strip; he worked and lived in other countries. For many years my mother and younger siblings lived with him.

My mother had four years of schooling and is literate; in those times, girls rarely went to school. But my father is illiterate. Since he found no work in the Gaza Strip, my father first left to work in Germany in 1964. His brother, who was already in Germany, sent my father a visa to be a guest-worker, and once my father began to work he regularly sent money to support us. But the money was not much, and my mother was always seeking ways to make ends meet. She would sew her clothes and ours, including our school uniforms. She taught us to raise rabbits and hens at home and sell them to earn money. Mother was very strict in her educational approach and punished us when we were naughty or did not fulfill her expectations.

At first, my father would visit us once a year. After the 1967 war, however, he came to visit for a longer period and wanted to resettle in the Gaza Strip. But after three months, Israeli military officers came and ordered him to leave the area. He had not been in the Gaza Strip when the Israeli army occupied the area; consequently, he had not received an identity card from the Israeli authorities. Israel issued identity cards for the Palestinians living in the Gaza Strip right after the June 1967 war. According to the official Israeli view, my father was not a resident of the Gaza Strip.

As a result of this Israeli military policy, my father had to leave to Egypt; from there he somehow renewed his visa for Germany and returned there to work. What is more, even after he became established as a guest-worker in Germany, the Israeli military still did not give him permission to visit the Gaza Strip. Because of this situation, my mother decided to join my father in Germany. In 1972, when I was twelve years old, she traveled there with my three younger sisters; they stayed there with my father for more than five years. After six years, however, my family had to leave Germany, because my father had been fired from his job and found no work. He did receive unemployment insurance but felt uncomfortable not working. In addition, the eldest of my sisters, who was with him, was fourteen years old and my father, who is conservative, did not want her to grow up in the liberal atmosphere of Germany. The family moved to Libya, where my father found work as a truck driver in a construction firm; he worked there from 1978 to 1981.

While my family was abroad, I remained in the Gaza Strip, together with Ziad, who was a year and a half older than I. We were excellent pupils in school, and the family decided that moving us from Gaza would be nonbeneficial to our education. Hence, since the fourth grade I have lived with my uncle and aunt. It turned out to be true that my sisters' education suffered because of their traveling from country to country. Yet for me, growing up without my mother and father, and without most of my immediate family, was difficult. Quite often the cruelty of the Israeli occupation also made my life miserable. Hence, I can say that I experienced quite a few moments of misery during my childhood and youth.

During my high school years, in the Awda Secondary School for girls in Abasan, I became involved in political activity. My views were different from those of most of my classmates. For instance, when I was fifteen years old I tried, together with other girls, to organize our class to leave our school and demonstrate on Land Day, which commemorates the seizing of our land by Israelis. When I was sixteen years old, after a student was killed by the Israeli soldiers I urged my classmates to go out and demonstrate against the occupation. We indeed demonstrated and angered the Israelis. They came to my grandfather, who was prominent in the Abasan community, and warned him to silence me, because they did not want to arrest me. My uncle spoke to me on this matter, and I answered rudely that his approach was a manner of collaborating with the Israelis.

I believe that many young Palestinian men, including Salem, my future husband, admired my political activities. Aside from the first incident that I mentioned, my uncle, in whose house I lived, also supported me. He understood that I must pursue my own way in our struggle for freedom from the Israeli occupation, and he did not stand in my way. He perceived that he also had participated in forming my character, and I believe that he saw that what I was doing was just and correct. When other members of the family criticized my political activities, he stood up for me, rejecting their criticism.

At times, other members of my extended family suffered because of my political activities. As a response to one of the demonstrations of high school girl students that I had organized, the Israelis decided to arrest me during the demonstration. They sent an Arab policeman, who was a known collaborator, to arrest me while the Israeli soldiers broke up the demonstration. But when we fled, the Arab policeman mistook my cousin, who resembles me and was running behind me, for Tahani. He arrested her. She stayed in jail overnight but was released on bail; she was charged with participating in an illegal demonstration. She told us that they had wanted to arrest Tahani, who, they stated, was inciting the girl students to demonstrate against the Israeli occupation.

During this period, even though I was often active against the Israeli occupation, I was not affiliated with any Palestinian political organization. Many acts of defiance engaged me. I worked with some male youths of my age in writing leaflets against the occupation and distributing them at night. We also wrote graffiti against the occupation on walls in Abasan. My uncle trusted me wholeheartedly. He knew very well that if I went out at night, it was because I was firmly committed to the Palestinian struggle for freedom and not because of a love affair. I also trusted him. If a young man sent me a love letter, I immediately showed it to my uncle. When I was seventeen years old, a teacher who liked me said that he would like to meet with me to talk. I told him to ask my uncle for permission, but he never asked. Thus, there was an atmosphere of trust between my uncle's family and me. He did not allow his own daughter to go out at night unless she went with me. This trust allowed me, often, to meet in my uncle's house with young men who were committed to working for the Palestinian cause.

While in high school, I was also known for my support of the poor people in our family and society. This attitude led to my being criticized by some of the rich people in our family. But members of my immediate neighborhood and family always rejected such criticism. I believe that my immediate family and neighborhood were liberal; hence, I had no problem sitting in the company of young men or even much older men and discussing different problems, even the problems of love. I was respected by all of them. They probably sensed that my firm rejection of the Israeli occupation was a result of my own thinking and way of life, and that aroused much respect.

According to my memories, even as a child I was against the Israeli occupation of the Gaza Strip when it commenced in 1967. I cannot put my finger on when I decided to fight against the Israeli occupation. I do remember my anger and my sorrow that after the Israeli occupation in 1967—when I was seven years old—we no longer feasted, as before, on our feast days of El Adha and El Fiter. In 1966, I wore a new dress for the feast and received many presents. But in 1967, since families were often separated as my family was, and because of the dejected mood of being under surveillance by an occupying army, we did not feast as in former years. Under Israeli occupation, the holidays had lost their joy.

When I was seventeen years old, my brother Ziad finished high school with very high grades; he wished to continue his studies. However, he was not offered a scholarship to study at a university in Egypt. Ziad was also an activist like me, but neither he nor I were affiliated with any of the Palestinian political factions. We soon learned that sons of martyrs who had fought against Israel, with much lower grades than my brother, were offered a university scholarship. Ziad was very sad at this decision, and I was angry at the way the Palestine Liberation Organization (PLO) allocated funds. I recognized that there was little justice in the way the PLO distributed resources to the Palestinian people, and I rebelled against its institutions. I also started to learn and think about the different factions of the PLO: the Fatah, headed by Yasser Arafat, whom we call Abu Ammar; the Popular Front for the Liberation of Palestine (PFLP); and the Democratic Front for the Liberation of Palestine (DFLP). I also learned a bit about Marxism and felt close to the PFLP which believed in Marxist-Communist principles.

My secondary school studies in the Gaza Strip ended in 1979. My family came for a visit and I returned with them to Libya to study for a year at a school of fashion design for women. Ziad traveled to Lebanon to study at a university there. In Libya, I decided to get married in 1980 to my cousin, Salem Abu Daqa, who was also my father's partner. He is ten years older than I. Salem and I met a few times and decided together to get married; it was not a traditionally arranged match. In the spring of 1981, Salem and I decided to return to the Gaza Strip. That was my only condition to getting married to him; I firmly wanted to live in the Gaza Strip. But we decided to remain in Libya for another year or more, or so we thought.

In 1981, there was a dispute between Abu Ammar and Muammar El Qaddafi; in response, Qaddafi issued a general statement ordering all Palestinian laborers to leave Libya. My father refused to leave and believed that he would not be deported. He was not affiliated with the Fatah but with the Democratic Front for the Liberation of Palestine; he thought that the order applied to people who were faithful to Arafat. But in the late summer of 1982, he and all my family, including Salem and me, were suddenly given twenty-four hours to leave Libya. One result was that my family had to leave behind many of their acquired goods. My father sold his car, but the Libyans took all the furniture in the house. We all flew to Cyprus and arrived there during the period of the Israeli-Lebanese war and the Sabra and Shatila massacre.

During the 1982 Israeli-Lebanese war, Israeli army units surrounded Sabra and Shatila, two refugee camps near Beirut. Later they allowed the Lebanese Christian militias to enter Sabra and Shatila and commit an atrocious massacre of hundreds of Palestinian refugees who resided in the camps. The Israeli army did not allow the Palestinian refugees to flee. Hundreds of Palestinian refugees of all ages were massacred in the two camps.

After three days in Cyprus, Salem and I took a boat to Haifa and from there we took a car to the Gaza Strip. My father did not know where to go from Cyprus. After two weeks, he decided to send the family to the Gaza Strip and to try his luck in Syria. My mother and sisters took a boat to Haifa and joined us in Abasan, while my father flew to Syria. The Syrians did not allow him to stay, and he traveled to Jordan and from there to Saudi Arabia. But after a few months, since he had no resident visa, he was deported from Saudi Arabia to Egypt. He was stranded in Egypt for some months; finally he received a visa to come to Morocco and work there raising chickens. He stayed in Morocco from 1983 until 1993, and during this period the Israeli authorities did not allow him to visit the Gaza Strip. My mother and younger siblings lived with him in Morocco most of the time.

My father received his first visiting permit to come to the Gaza Strip in 1993, after the Oslo Agreement and a short time before the Israelis left. He was sixty-five years old. Since he believed that the changes brought about by the Oslo Agreement would allow him to stay in the Gaza Strip, he sold his chicken farm and left Morocco. But the Israeli security officials who checked his luggage at the Rafah border terminal found a bullet in one of his suitcases and tore up his visa. Because he had no place of residence, he was held in the airport in Egypt for a while, and finally my uncle in Morocco arranged for him to return to Morocco. Only after much lobbying and intervention of the press was he again issued a visiting permit; he arrived in the Gaza Strip in 1994. He remained in the Gaza Strip without an identity card for five years, until 1999. Only then did the Israeli security authority issue him an identity card and permit him to officially reunite with his family. He is seventy-four years old and has no income. Ziad, who when I traveled to Libya in 1981 received a scholarship to study medicine in Germany, became a medical doctor. He became a German citizen, lives and practices medicine in Berlin, and supports our parents.

After returning from Libya, I decided to continue my political activity against the Israeli occupation. At first I worked with women members of the Communist Party, specifically in gathering money to set up kindergartens and rejuvenating their women's movement. I was surprised to find that many young women wanted to marry someone who lived and worked outside of the Gaza Strip, say in Morocco or Saudi Arabia, where salaries were higher and they could live at a higher standard of living. I started organizing groups to educate the women that we must struggle for a better future for the Palestinian people here in Palestine. During this period I was affiliated with the PFLP, as was my husband, Salem. But after a while, we felt that the PFLP did not relate to our activities. Hence, when people from the DFLP contacted me and asked me to join their party, I agreed.

When I became a mother in 1982, I learned that I am not similar to many mothers. My energies are not directed to being very affectionate but rather to being practical. I gave birth to three daughters and two sons. My eldest daughter, Seba, is nineteen years old and my youngest son, Muhammad, is nine years old. My not being overaffectionate in my relations with my children may have to do with my own childhood and youth, which was not spent with my immediate family. I had to grow up with my own family abroad and live as a conservative girl who cared for the reputation of my uncle. As a child, Mother's Day was an especially sad day, because all the girls had mothers with whom they lived, while my mother was not in the Gaza Strip. Thus, although I am dedicated to the well-being of my children, and I work to provide for their needs and help them to fulfill their wishes, they do not receive much overt affection from me. Salem, like other Arab men, believes that affection should come from women; he did not compensate our children for my lack of expressions of affection.

When Salem and I returned from Libya in 1982, we decided to work in agriculture; we set up a dunam and a half of plastic agricultural greenhouses. In the greenhouses we grew cucumbers, tomatoes, and peppers. On our other land we grew vegetables. Our first year was very successful financially. I liked working with plants and enjoyed seeing them grow; farming still brings me joy. But in the third year there were many closures of the border with Israel, and we could not sell the vegetables; we lost much money.

At the end of 1983, I became a partner in a small sewing workshop in which workers sewed clothes which were to be exported, mainly to Israel. We worked directly with Israeli dealers in clothes. I had studied fashion design and had worked as a teacher of sewing in Libya. I had two other partners, both from Gaza City. We employed between ten and fifteen workers. My job was to design the clothes and to manage the business. Usually I worked from eight in the morning until four in the afternoon. Infrequently, when there were orders to fill or other problems, I would work until the late evening hours. Our first orders were for winter jackets and coats; later there were orders for all kinds of clothes.

I worked in the workshop for about four years and it was financially successful. Personally, however, I was not good at taking care of my own money. When needy people asked me for financial support, I gave generously, especially to members of my extended family. The result was that when troubles began with the Israeli security branches, Salem and I had not established ourselves in a good home; we still lived in a rather small apartment, with used furniture. When our major troubles began, we did not have money left from the good years.

In 1987, around the time the intifada started, I had already extended my political activities within the DFLP to the entire Gaza Strip. Among these activities were organizing women's groups to establish kindergartens and setting up women's cooperatives where they could work and earn money. We also had groups of women who met in order to raise their awareness concerning the injustice of the Israeli military occupation of the Gaza Strip. The Israeli occupation forces, especially the Shabak, the Israeli security service, started to make life difficult for me. They sent collaborators who joined our organization and gathered material about us. They sent women to try to seduce Salem. In these endeavors they failed—but we learned to be careful.

I also believe that the Israeli security service convinced our Palestinian partners to withdraw one after the other from our partnership in the sewing workshop. Salem and I became the sole owners of the factory. I also noticed that there was always someone trailing me, both when I went to the workshop and when I engaged in my activities for the DFLP. Salem and I continued to work in the factory, and it went quite well until the Israeli intelligence started to send us indirect threats through acquaintances. They also may have made it hard for us to find Israeli buyers for the clothes that we produced, which made it difficult to work regular shifts. We understood that our situation was becoming even more adverse when the Israelis denied my request for permission to travel abroad.

When the intifada broke out in December 1987, I started organizing women to support the wounded and assist them to get the medical treatment that they deserved. We also helped the families of Palestinians whom the Israeli military had imprisoned and the martyrs who were killed by Israeli soldiers. In addition, we tried to make sure that children had milk and food during long periods of harsh Israeli military curfew, when our people were not allowed to go out of their homes. All this activity was linked to our constantly speaking with women and trying to raise their political awareness about the evils of the Israeli military occupation. We women worked independently, without receiving orders from the leadership of the DFLP, who were situated outside Israel. I belonged to the leadership committee of the DFLP in the Gaza Strip, and there was a leadership committee for the West Bank. I was one of the few women in a top leadership role.

The response of the Israeli army came quickly. They arrested me and closed our sewing workshop. The official reason for my arrest and for the closing of the workshop was that we were sewing Palestinian flags. I don't think that they found flags, but they said they did. While I was jailed in Ramleh prison, they told my husband that no one was allowed to work in the sewing workshop. Thus the Israelis extinguished our sole source of income.

My period of incarceration made me quite well known in the Gaza Strip. Not many women were jailed by the Israeli authorities. The Israeli lawyers who represented me were Leah Zemel and Tamar Peleg. The court convened in Ramleh Prison inside Israel. I was sentenced to six months administrative detention, which meant that I was not put on trial for any specific crime but merely jailed because I was supposedly dangerous to the forces of the Israeli military occupation.

After a few days in the Israeli women's prison, I learned that I was pregnant. I told the Ramleh prison authorities that I was pregnant; they seemed annoyed. They sent an Israeli social worker to speak to me. She asked me why I wanted a child and added that I might spend a long time in jail, sentenced to repeated periods of administrative detention, which would not be good for the child. I responded that the pregnancy was unplanned, I learned about it in prison, and that I had no intention to abort the child.

A week later my husband visited me in prison. The prison director summoned both of us to her office. She told my husband that I was pregnant and that I had to abort my child. Her reasons were that there was a possibility of extending my detention in prison and that being pregnant and raising a child in prison would be very difficult and very tiring for me. She told my husband that an abortion was for my good and that raising a baby in prison was wrong. I told the prison director that I wanted my child, even if they did not want it. I stated clearly that I wanted to give birth and that I refused to undergo an abortion.

After that a weird medical process began. Three times a prison nurse took a blood sample from me. They told me that the blood samples revealed that I was weak, and they gave me medicine. I believed them and took the medicine. After that, they wanted to take additional blood samples. I became suspicious and told them that they had taken blood three times and there was no need to take a blood sample again. A nurse told me to take additional medicine, and added that they would see whether I would abort. I notified her that I did not want an abortion, and she said that it was not my business. I took the medicine again and suddenly I felt that I was bleeding.

I went to the clinic and the nurse phoned the doctor to ask for instructions. He instructed her to lay me on my abdomen and to put hot water on my back and abdomen. She brought the hot water and the moment she started putting a towel soaked in hot water on my back and abdomen, an elderly Arab woman prisoner advised me that what they were doing to me was dangerous. She said that the hot water would cause me to abort my child. I did not believe her and said that they were following a doctor's orders. She replied that they were endangering my life. I answered that I did not believe that the Israelis could reach such a degree of cruelty. I added that there is a separation between the army policy and the medical doctors, and that it was not conceivable that doctors could undertake such brutal practices.

But the elderly woman prisoner spoke the truth. When they put hot water on my back, I started to bleed and abort my child. After that I received appropriate medical treatment, but I was forced to abort against my will. In short, I accuse the Israeli prison administration of causing my abortion.

When my family came to visit me a few days after I aborted my child, I demanded that they send the Red Cross to investigate my forced abortion. A few weeks later, representatives of the Red Cross came to investigate my complaint. On that specific day, however, the clinic was closed, and all the persons who worked in the clinic were unavailable. As far as I remember, that was the only day the clinic was closed. A day or two after the visit of the Red Cross representatives, I was taken to court for a discussion of my case. This time I represented myself, without a lawyer. Members of my family were present, and after the discussion in court they returned home. The court gave no verdict that day, and I was returned to prison. That evening, however, the prison authorities called me and told me that I was released and could go home. Two days later, I learned from the newspaper that the court had not decided to release me from prison; but still I was released. Later I asked a lawyer to sue the prison authorities for causing my abortion, but there was not enough hard evidence to sue them, so I gave up. My period of imprisonment was around two and a half months.

After my release from prison, I resumed my work for Palestinian freedom from Israeli occupation. The Israeli authorities responded to my activities by coming to our house and beating and arresting Salem. A Shabak officer, who was called Abu Zayed, accompanied by a squad of Israeli soldiers, entered our house when I was not present and beat up Salem in front of our children. After the beating they arrested him. In jail they continued to beat and torture him. They told Salem that they were beating him because his wife did not learn the lesson they wanted to teach her when she was arrested.

Salem was incarcerated in the Ansar II jail in Gaza City for thirty-seven days without being charged with any wrongdoing. Finally, Salem was released and forced to pay $1,500 bail. Even though he was never charged with any wrongdoing, the bail was never returned to us. Furthermore, the Israeli authorities never investigated or interrogated Salem; they jailed him and beat him as a punishment for my activities. At that time we had very little money. We raised the $1,500 for Salem's bail by taking loans from friends and family members.

When speaking with one of the Israeli officers during my husband's imprisonment, I told him that the Israelis had made me famous. Formerly, I was a simple woman, but now Tahani was a famous figure—a freedom fighter who had aborted her child in an Israeli prison because of their harsh treatment of her. My involvement in the struggle for freedom propelled me into a leadership role, and I became a member of the DFLP Party's leadership in the Gaza Strip. My leadership role included great responsibilities, and the people trusted me. In assuming this role, I strongly felt that we Palestinians, as a people, have rights, and we must develop ourselves and fight for these rights. We must stop depending on politicians in Arab countries to bring us our rights, but must fight on our own to attain them.

An additional result of my return to political activity was that threats against me by the Israeli authorities increased. Every so often, a squad of Israeli soldiers, led by a Shabak officer, would enter our house in the middle of the night to seek me. They did not find me. I was aware that they were looking for me and wanted to beat me severely; hence I slept every night in a different house and never at home. At times, when the Israeli soldiers did not find me at my home, they would become angry and frustrated and would vent their anger on our furniture, breaking it. During this difficult period, Salem firmly supported my political activities.

My links with the United Leadership of the Intifada were strong. In the United Leadership of the Intifada were representatives from four major Palestinian factions. The first six leaflet-communiques that the DFLP published were handed by me, first, to the leaders of the Fatah movement. We signed them the United Leadership, and in the southern area of the Gaza Strip, the leaflets were distributed by women in groups that I led. We women traveled disguised, at times wearing traditional clothes and veils. We would knock at every door, and when we heard someone coming, we would leave the leaflet and vanish. We tried to reach every house, since we wanted to encourage all our people to join the intifada. We were very careful in distributing these leaflets and were never caught by the Israeli military.

During these months of intense activity against the Israeli occupation, there was one incident in which an Israeli convoy of soldiers could have shot me. It occurred during the extended curfew that was imposed upon all Palestinians after the Israelis killed the Fatah leader, Abu Jihad, in Tunis. We learned that people in the Khan Yunis refugee camp needed milk for their children and medicine for people who were ill, and decided to distribute milk and medicine despite the curfew. Quite late at night, two small trucks carrying milk and medicine brought us, a group of women, to a hidden place close to the refugee camp. Each woman took some supplies and went to a different neighborhood of houses to ask who needed supplies and distribute the supplies that she had to the needy.

As I was walking, I entered a wide street and saw an Israeli army convoy of jeeps and trucks, with searchlights mounted on some of the jeeps, enter from the opposite direction. There were no entrances to the houses along the street, and I was gripped by fear since it was evident that the soldiers in the convoy would shoot anyone moving. Suddenly I saw a large, standing metal plate stuck in the ground, behind which I could hide. The tall metal plate was all that remained of an old kiosk which had been used to sell falafel. I quickly hid behind the standing metal plate. As the patrol passed, their searchlight illuminated the metal plate behind which I stood, but they did not discern me. I am confident that if they had seen me, they would have opened fire—without asking any questions.

Our economic situation during the intifada was difficult. Our workshop was closed and we had no source of income. When I was offered money by the PLO, I got angry and said that we are fighting and struggling for freedom and should not take money for our efforts. We lived with members of our family who had an income, and they fed us. We ate from the produce of the land, mainly vegetables which grew in Gaza. Thus, after I got out of prison we had food but no cash. I remember that my husband's sister decided to get married, and I wanted to buy a new dress for the wedding. Since we had no cash, I sold some of my gold, the gold that every Arab bride receives from the groom before she gets married, and bought the dress. In short, we lived very frugally during the intifada, relying on the support of members of my family. I continue to live modestly, and although we now have money, I have no jewels and have not bought back my gold.

I have maintained good relations with all political parties in the Gaza Strip, including members of the Islamic Resistance Movement, the Hamas. I respect views, feelings, and ideologies that differ from my own, and recognize that they reflect different parts of our society. During the intifada, the Israeli authorities attempted to create divisions between certain political parties and me. They once had some Palestinian youths write graffiti warning all people not to deal with Tahani since she was irreligious. The graffiti was signed "Hamas." After some inquiries, and after questioning the youths who had written the graffiti, it was evident that they had collaborated with the Israeli authorities. In general, collaborators knew that I was their enemy.

Much later a few collaborators confessed that they had tried to shoot me but had not succeeded in finding the appropriate opportunity. Once they had aimed a gun at me from a window, but some people came and stood between me and the gun, and they lost their chance to shoot me. Another time a group of about ten masked men came to our house and wanted to take me from my home. They came into the shop in front of our home and then knocked at our door. They said they were from Fatah, but it was evident that they were lying. The people of Abasan supported me, including those from the Fatah, and the men suddenly lacked the courage to face me and went away. Later it was learned that the leader of the group was a collaborator with Israel; some time later he was killed by the Palestinian national activists.

Although I belonged to the DFLP, I worked first and foremost for my people, which often meant working hand in hand with Fatah members. For instance, during the intifada there were times when the DFLP sent me money so as to support our members. But I felt that there were members of Fatah whose families needed the money much more urgently, and I gave the money to them. The same is true for all other material help that I received to distribute; I often gave it to members of the Fatah. Thus, when a Fatah man was wounded in our area, I was called in to help. The reason was that the doctors trusted me and immediately came when I requested that one of them come to treat the wound. In addition, I arranged safe places for the wounded from all parties to be hidden and treated by doctors and health personnel. Thus, all parties and many people knew that they could receive aid at my house, and they came to us; often there were members of the Islamic parties among them. These activities, in all segments of our society, required that I dress more conservatively, which meant wearing a long dress and covering my hair.

In 1991, when the peace process began with the meetings in Madrid, the DFLP split into two factions, one supporting the peace process and the other against it. Yasser Abed Rabu led the faction that demanded a renewal of the DFLP and support for the peace process. I was one of the leading figures in the renewal faction and worked hard convincing people to support the PLO and the peace process. The majority of the people in the Gaza Strip who had adhered to the DFLP joined the renewal faction. The women's groups with whom I was in contact all supported the peace process and the renewal faction of the DFLP.

It was very important to avoid a split in the women's groups of the DFLP in the Gaza Strip, because a split would harm our social and communal activities. We were involved in supporting twenty-five kindergartens and leading more than thirty women's training centers. In addition, we supported what we called four productive projects, in which women earned money. Among these projects was a child nutrition center in the Palestinian refugee camp El Burej; a production center for folklore mats in Khan Yunis; a cooperative in Abasan which baked biscuits and produced and marketed milk products; and a goat farm. All the projects were run by women.

I was not involved in the military activities of the DFLP, but in the popular political activities. Within the DFLP, there was complete separation between these activities. The reason for this separation was that those who were active in popular politics, like myself, could be arrested any day. Hence, it was better that we know nothing of the military activities. Indeed, I knew nothing. I was also much more interested in building up the spirit of our people, teaching them to live correctly in freedom and justice, than in military activities against the Israeli army. Perhaps I should add that after seeing Israeli soldiers kill fellow Palestinians, I reached the stage where I could kill an Israeli soldier. But, on the other hand, I felt disgusted when Palestinians bombed buses and indiscriminately killed women and children. I did not see such actions as military achievements.

What was unique to the DFLP was that there were many women in leadership roles. In other organizations there were no women who served in the leadership council. However, despite my leadership role, after the 1991 Madrid peace summit meetings, I decided in 1992 to stop my political activities. I felt that the battle for the freedom of the Palestinian people had become unclean.

Let me give an example of what I mean by an unclean approach to our fight for freedom. During the intifada, I was a leading figure in the party. My responsibilities included participation in the leadership council. But when the intifada ended and many men who had been active in the party got out of prison, they told me that I had no place in the leadership council. They were polite and said: Thank you very much, Tahani, for what you have done. But, they added, your role now is merely to head the women's division of the party. I told them that I had quite a bit of experience in leading our struggle and saw no reason to leave the leadership council. But the men insisted that women were not to be included in the leadership roles. This chauvinist approach angered me, and I resigned from all political activity.

Perhaps I should be more explicit. The Madrid summit brought about a struggle for power in the DFLP. Many of the men who now fought for power in the party had been cowards during the intifada; they had fled while we women organized activities against the Israelis. Now these cowards were among the men who notified me that since I was a woman, I had to leave the leadership council. In short, the struggle for power in the party disgusted me and I decided to leave. I wanted to serve my people and work with them directly so as to enhance their everyday existence. I did not want to struggle within the party for a post of leadership.

I informed the party that I did not want to work for them. There were attempts to convince me to remain in the party. I was invited to meet the party leadership in Jordan, and it was agreed there that I would be one of a three-member party leadership committee in the Gaza Strip. But when I returned to the Gaza Strip from Jordan, the agreement was not implemented because other people refused to give up their posts. A hornet's nest of problems erupted and many people opposed my belonging to the leadership. I can state categorically that those people who opposed my leadership cared more about securing their own posts than about the national struggle. These people were acting according to a trend that has become common in the Palestinian Authority, whereby people attain prominent positions by being sycophants and not because of their merits.

Another reason I felt bad about being politically active was because of what had happened when the DFLP split into two parties: those who supported the Oslo Agreement and those who opposed it. There was much deceit and violence between members of the different factions of the DFLP. For instance, I was beaten by former members of my party, who now belong to another faction. Unfortunately, I also participated in these aggressive activities, although not violently; I also defamed former party members so as to convince people to work with our pro-peace faction. The entire situation of deceit and aggression made me sick. I became quite disenchanted with politics.

However, my main reason for stopping to be active in the DFLP, with whom I felt linked spiritually, was my discovery that after the Oslo Agreement, the leaders of the party lacked an overall strategy for bringing freedom, peace, and well-being to our people. The role of the person who chooses to be politically active is to help the people improve their lot, educate them, and show them how to communicate together democratically. But when the intifada stopped and the Oslo Agreement was signed, few leaders assumed such a responsibility. They were more interested in ensuring their political positions than in working for the people. This, I believe, was the major reason that when the Palestinian Authority arrived in the Gaza Strip in 1993, I stopped being politically active.

For me personally, becoming aware of the true political situation and deciding to resign from political activity brought great frustration. I had been called an iron woman during the intifada. After resigning from political activity, I felt like a balloon whose air had been released; all that remained was a piece of rubber. I understood that I must study and broaden my horizons, and I did go to the university. I enrolled in the El Kuds Palestinian Open University in the Gaza Strip; after studying for three years I received a bachelor's degree in management and marketing. During that period, a group of women to which I belonged started to think about establishing programs for women. I did not establish links with the Palestinian Authority, because I felt that they had chosen a path that would not lead to a just peace. They spoke slogans and did not relate to the terrible reality of injustice and lack of freedom that prevailed in the Gaza Strip.

After the arrival of the Palestinian Authority in 1994, many men continued to do their utmost to marginalize me as a woman and leader of women. Among those who resented my leadership role were some men of my extended family.

Four years ago during our feast, the men of my extended family decided to go to President Yasser Arafat and express their best holiday wishes to him. A few of the women in my extended family, including myself, decided to join the delegation. The head of the delegation asked all of us not to speak directly to Abu Ammar. If we wanted to convey something, we should present it to him, the head of the delegation, and he would tell Abu Ammar. Well, it didn't happen that way.

When we arrived, in the speech that he gave after the initial formalities, Abu Ammar stated that we people of the eastern area of the Gaza Strip were good people. At that point I interrupted his speech. I said, "Pardon me for interrupting. The people may be good, but currently the environment and the conditions in which we live are destructive of that good." Abu Ammar answered, "You will remain good." I replied: "You should come and see what is going on. You should see the difficulties the people have in their daily existence." One of the aides standing near Arafat said, "Abu Ammar knows everything." I answered: "What Abu Ammar knows he sees through your eyes and not through his own eyes. If he will see through his own eyes, the situation will change." At the end of the meeting, when we were parting, Arafat gave me a sweet. But the head of the delegation was furious with me for speaking out on my own. He went to my father and complained about my behavior. After that, when the men decided to go to meet Abu Ammar, they never informed me.

I believe that my response at that meeting was appropriate and is still true. Many of the decisions are made by the people who surround and serve Abu Ammar and not by him. Some of the reasons for such a situation are his age and his health problems. I believe that if Abu Ammar was in good health, he would firmly struggle against many of the difficulties that are happening to us—in the economy, in financial management of our country, in internal politics, and in the international political arena, including our relations with Israel. For decades, Abu Ammar struggled relentlessly for the freedom of the Palestinian people. Indeed, all of his life Abu Ammar worked very hard and honestly for the Palestinian people, and I am not blaming him for the difficult situation in the Gaza Strip now. But I do question the decisions and the policies of the people who surround him. Often these decisions and policies, which they convince Abu Ammar to accept, are ruinous for our people.

Unfortunately, we are quite uninformed about the true state of affairs in which we find ourselves. We do not know about the external pressures that are imposed on Abu Ammar. We do not know the philosophy which guides his decisions. Consequently, it is hard for me to evaluate what is currently happening. I see what is happening, but giving a full evaluation is difficult. I see that I was a citizen here before the Palestinian Authority arrived, and with their arrival some things changed. There are some changes on the ground. The streets are clean. Houses, roads, and schools are built. People feel secure and know that the Israelis can no longer forbid them, say, to go to the sea. But we also see rich people who have become ostentatious with their wealth. Thus, you can see a private car that awaits a nine-year-old girl to take her to and from school. Such an ostentatious display of wealth angers me.

A few years ago, we all lived miserably, oppressed by the Israelis. But there was a sense of community. Now since some people have become very wealthy, while others still live in poverty, the sense of community is being eroded. I do not know the reasons for the changes, but many people are disappointed. I do not see the problem as being rooted in the distinction between indigenous inhabitants of the Gaza Strip and those who came from abroad. We, the Palestinians, are one people, distinct from the other Arab peoples. We must all act morally in our ongoing struggle for freedom and a good life.

As an understatement I would say that the Oslo Agreement and many of its results have not fulfilled our expectations. Many of the problems that we face are due to the ongoing Israeli occupation and oppression, which is performed by means other than direct rule by an occupying military force. The Israelis make many unjust demands upon the Palestinian Authority, and when our leaders fulfill these demands they disappoint the people and erode their own authority. Furthermore, quite a few sections of the original agreements that we signed, such as the Paris Economic Protocol, were unjust and brought additional suffering to many Palestinians.

One of my primary current concerns is to earn money so as to support my family. My daughter, Seba, will soon go to the university, and that requires money. My husband has no job. We have stopped farming because of Israeli policies, which do not allow us to market our crops successfully outside of the Gaza Strip; inside the Gaza Strip the prices for agricultural produce are very low. We sold the sewing workshop and used the money to live. Currently, I have a job with a project sponsored by the government of Denmark that educates Palestinians living in the central area of the Gaza Strip for a life of democracy, while helping them better their environment. My salary supports my family; I also work as a volunteer in community associations.

My major worry is about the Palestinian people. When we supported the peace process, we were skeptical and said that at least it would improve the image of the Palestinian people abroad. We would no longer be described as terrorists who reject peaceful solutions to disagreements. We should strive for peace, even if peace might never prevail. People should know that today Israeli policies are the major hindrance to peace. But during the peace process, our spirit of community and desire to seek justice has deteriorated. People are interested in bettering themselves materially and do not care much about other people's problems. Before this change in attitudes, many people helped the poor and the hungry. Now very little help is forthcoming. The same is true about me. My salary was once $200 a month and I used to help many people. Now my salary, which is exceptional among Palestinians, is $1,600 a month, and I feel that it is not enough for what my family needs.

Lately, we also discern within Palestine quite a few manipulative and corrupt people who have obtained power and act wrongly. These developments arouse my concern about our existence as a people. We should firmly reject corruption and help every person feel his or her value as a unique individual. We should educate the children, the coming generation of Palestinians, to strive for justice, equality, and democracy, and help them overcome their sad experiences that are a result of their family's suffering. My colleagues and I, in the projects in which I am involved, are working in this direction, and we believe that we have made some progress.

One of the reasons that I did not seek work in the Palestinian Authority after Yasser Arafat arrived in Gaza was the method of obtaining work. Unfortunately, this method was brought to Gaza by the PLO leadership. It required that the person seeking work find recommendations in the circle close to Arafat. Such an approach to seeking work was not something I could stomach. I wanted to be hired for a job on the basis of my personal qualifications, not because of my connections with certain persons in power. Unfortunately, to this day, the methods of deciding to employ people in the Palestinian Authority rarely take into account a person's qualifications.

Let me say a bit more about the project in which I currently work, sponsored by the government of Denmark. A major goal of the project is to help us to build a civil community in three refugee camps in the central area of the Gaza Strip. The government of Denmark has allotted millions of dollars to each of these camps for building community projects. There are a few conditions that must be fulfilled before the camp receives the money. These conditions are: The community should convene, determine its priorities, and set up a democratic organization that will oversee the spending of the money. This overseeing organization must ensure transparency and that the money received goes to those priorities that, according to the community's decision, would best benefit the residents of the refugee camps. An example of one of the priorities decided upon in one of the camps was the establishing and running of kindergartens.

My responsibilities in this project include educating members of each community to undertake this democratic and communal responsibility; I am also responsible for making sure that the conditions set by the government of Denmark are met. I work twelve hours a day, so I am not very well aware of many of the details of the political situation in the Gaza Strip. I do have congenial relations with the institutions of the Palestinian Authority, especially with the Ministry of Local Government. People in all the ministries with which I interact respect me and my work.

My children also respect my work and are proud of their mother, who differs from other women of her age group and is energetic, politically active, and a bit famous. They are delighted when other children at school talk about my activities. My husband is also very supportive. I know that it is difficult for him since he is unemployed and stays at home. He greatly respects me and encourages me to go forward in my work and struggles. He does not feel that my work and success diminish his respect or disparage him.

Looking back at my activities in helping promote the freedom of Palestinian women and struggling to better our society during the years since the end of the intifada brings me some satisfaction. As early as 1991, a number of women groups to which I belonged expressed great concern about the education of our children. We recognized that during the intifada, the children had lost many months of schooling. What is more, when they were out of school, the children had engaged in aggressive actions against Israeli soldiers. Frequently, we perceived, this aggressive behavior had infiltrated into other aspects of their lives, including their behavior in schools. Furthermore, when the schools were open, such behavior—albeit by a few children—created problems for all the children.

Our first act was to establish in Khan Yunis a Club for Children that served the city and the adjoining refugee camp. In the club, we attempted to help children and youths regain their childhood. Five of us women worked at the club as volunteers and often supported the activities from our own meager financial means. A French organization called The Association of World's Refugees and Children wanted to help the children of the intifada, and they gave us some financial support. Once the club was set up and perceived as an educational success, members of different political factions approached us and demanded that we be affiliated with them. Among other things, they wanted us to accept their decisions concerning the appointment of workers in the club. We refused and told them not to interfere in our educational work. They brought pressure. We were adamant. Finally, the polticians let us engage in our activities without their interference.

In 1995 we succeeded in making the Club for Children into a Non-Government Organization (NGO) called the Cultural and Free Thought Association. The Club for Children became a group of five centers which the association runs. There is the Hope Center which provides after-school education for children ages six through twelve. There is a Youth Club for ages twelve through seventeen. There is a Community Center dedicated to culture. There is a Unionist Women's Center which deals with women's rights. Finally there is a Center for Women's Health with a branch in El Bureij refugee camp and a branch in Khan Yunis. The Center for Women's Health is an institution that has had much success not only in Palestine but in many developing countries. The center deals with many areas of health such as raising women's consciousness about health, family planning, psychological counseling, and legal advice.

Today, the Cultural and Free Thought Association is very successful. We have a yearly budget of contributions to our Non-Government Organization of about one million dollars. There are sixty people employed in the administration and the various centers that we run. There are also twelve volunteers. I work as a volunteer, but when I have expenses they are paid by the association. The association also sponsors a loan office for women in the Gaza Strip. It endeavors to assist women who wish to undertake any kind of commercial project to earn money for themselves and their families.

Among my other current engagements, one additional activity should probably be mentioned. I participate in a Model Women Parliament of Israeli and Palestinian women who work for peace. Specifically, we work to upgrade the role of women in bringing a lasting peace. This project is funded by the government of The Netherlands, and we are in contact with a European parliamentary women's organization.

Chapter 4

Tawfik Abu Khousa

I was born in 1961 in Gaza City. I have eight brothers and five sisters. My parents are refugees who fled in 1948 to the Gaza Strip from the town of Isdood, which was in what is now the Israeli city of Ashdod. Near Isdood, they had land upon which there was a bustan of fig trees and other fruit trees. After my family arrived in the Gaza Strip, for the rest of his life my father was a day laborer. He worked in agriculture, especially in fruit picking, and also in construction of houses. My father no longer works. We brothers support our parents.

Until the ninth grade, I was a pupil in the UNWRA school in Rimal for children of refugees. It was tuition free. After that I studied in the Palestine High School for boys. There was a very small fee for high school tuition. After 1967, these schools were totally under Israeli rule. I wanted to continue my studies at the university level, but it didn't work out. At the secondary school level, I especially enjoyed learning history. I was fortunate to have a very good teacher, Salah Zacut, who taught us Arabic. In the ninth grade he loaned me Maxim Gorky's book *The Mother* and told me to read it. After I finished reading *The Mother*, throughout my high school years he continued to lend me books from his personal library to read. Every week or two I would read a book. Most of these books were oriented toward his beliefs in equality and freedom. Thus, I read about the struggles of the Communist Party in Bolivia and in Vietnam. During the years that I was in high school, the Communist Party was the largest party in the Gaza Strip.

At that time, it was quite common in our schools for teachers to be attracted to bright pupils; that is, pupils who succeeded in examinations and were interested in the subject that they taught. These teachers frequently assisted their successful pupils in their personal development. Teachers with Islamic beliefs also helped many pupils. In each class there were around fifty pupils, which made it very difficult for the teacher to educate. Hence, developing personal relations with a few of the talented pupils may have been one of the ways by which teachers tried to educate at least a few pupils.

I was never a staunch supporter of communism, but I learned much from reading the books that Zacut gave me. I understood the injustice done to me and my people. This injustice stemmed from the fact that, as Palestinians, my family and I were refugees, whose land had been taken from us by force. During that period, the communists in the Gaza Strip were free to pursue their political goals. This partial political freedom helped me decide, in 1977, when I was in the tenth grade, to work against the Israeli occupation. In this undertaking, I worked together with other youths who were patriots.

Using carbon paper, a group of us high school students would write and copy leaflets with declarations condemning the Israeli occupation. One of our first leaflets was before the second anniversary of Land Day; in the leaflet, we condemned the Israelis for confiscating land that belonged to the Palestinians. We did not sign the leaflets. We put four leaflets in each classroom, and I believe that our message reached most of the 1,700 students in Palestine High School. Since a sister of one of our group helped us copy the leaflets, she took some and distributed them in her high school for young women. (Boys and girls learn in separate schools throughout the Gaza Strip.) A few of the teachers assisted us in these activities, mainly by not reporting what we had done or by turning a blind eye to our words and deeds.

The leaflets that we distributed before Land Day were effective, because the next day the high school students organized a demonstration and marched against the occupation; they clashed with the Israeli soldiers. I am convinced that our statements and declarations encouraged the students to demonstrate against the Israeli occupation. My role in putting out the leaflets was significant. From early youth I had read many books and had a good command of Arabic; hence, I was doing most of the writing of these Palestinian patriotic declarations. The other students helped in copying the leaflets and distributing them at school during the night and in the street.

As we became more active, the teachers and the principal became aware of my leadership role in the activities against the Israelis. But, since I was on the school football (soccer) team and was a good student and friendly with the teachers and the administration, they quietly supported me. I remember one incident when the principal saved me from being arrested. It was in 1979 and the students of Palestine High School demonstrated against President Sadat of Egypt, who had decided to make peace with Israel. We felt that he was abandoning the Palestinian cause; we demonstrated and clashed with the Israeli army. During the clash, the soldiers shot in the air and also shot tear gas at us to disperse us. I was among the organizers of the demonstration. We wore masks during the demonstration so we could not be identified. Later, the army surrounded the Palestine High School and closed the entire area. They came into the school and arrested many students. They performed the arrests under the eyes of the principal and the military commander of Gaza City. At first, the soldiers tried to identify who had thrown rocks by looking at our hands, but we had all washed our hands. So they arrested students quite randomly. I was among those who were arrested.

When the principal saw me standing in the playground, guarded by the Israeli soldiers who had arrested me, near the military truck that was to take us to jail, he came up to me and asked, "What are you doing here?" I replied, "I've been arrested." The principal then slapped me in the face so hard that I reeled, and he ordered me to return immediately to the classroom. He turned to the Israeli commander and told him that he knew that I was not involved in any bad activities, that I was a star on their football team, and that I just wanted to be arrested with some of my friends. The commander agreed to my release and I returned to class. With that slap, the principal saved me from being imprisoned. He later appologized to me for having to use such tactics.

In 1979, I participated in the first major demonstration of high school students from many schools against the Israeli occupation. I don't remember the specific reason for that demonstration. We demonstrated at Omar El Mukhtar, which is the main central street in the city of Gaza. The Israeli army came and blocked off the area. Israeli soldiers then began shooting bullets into the air and tear gas into the crowd of students. I fled. Unfortunately, however, I fled into an alley in which stood an Israeli army jeep, which I had not noticed. Near the jeep stood at least six soldiers, and suddenly I found myself surrounded by them. They caught me and started beating me with their hands and kicking me. They forced me to lie in the back of the jeep and continued their beatings. They then tied my hands and, while driving the jeep to the jail, continued beating and kicking me as I lay there.

The soldiers serving in the Israeli army jail, to which I was taken, also beat me. I was never interrogated, just beaten five times in the jail. Every few hours I would be taken to an hour of beatings. Together with around fifty other pupils, I was charged with throwing stones. All fifty of us went through the same ordeal; every few hours we were beaten without ever being interrogated. Finally, there was a very quick trial for every one of us, and we were each fined between 100 and 150 lira and released.

When I completed secondary school in the summer of 1979, I wanted to continue my studies in Moscow. The Communist Party in the Gaza Strip had arranged that I receive a study stipend, and I had some friends who were already studying in Moscow. I applied for permission to leave the Gaza Strip and received an invitation to meet one of the representatives of the Shabak, the Israeli security service, in Gaza City. This representative of the Shabak was a red-headed man who said his name was Abu Vehal. He told me that he would not allow me to leave the Gaza Strip unless I agreed to become a collaborator who provided information for the Shabak. I firmly refused. I decided to apply again, but I did not receive permission to leave the Gaza Strip. I applied again and again and always received the same answer: Only if you become a collaborator will the Israeli security service allow you to leave the Gaza Strip. These continual refusals forced me to give up the idea of studying in Moscow.

Let me tell you a story that is not yet known. During the period that I was applying to leave for Moscow, in late 1980 or the early months of 1981, I was also active against the Israeli occupation, together with other youths. I was in one of two groups of youths who were affiliated with Fatah. One night at ten o'clock we smashed the windows of the branches of two Israeli central banks in Gaza City, Hapoalim Bank and Discount Bank. Alarms went off, the Israeli soldiers came, and there was shooting. But they arrived after we all had fled to the citrus groves that surround the city. We stayed in the orange groves until everything quieted down and returned to our homes at around 2:00 A.M.

I started to work as a day laborer in Israel and worked there for more than three years. I mainly worked in construction, in the cities of Tel Aviv and Ashdod. At times, I worked in agriculture in the Beer Sheva area. But I also started to be active in politics, against the Israeli occupation of Palestinian land. This situation of work during the day and political activities at night continued from 1980 until 1983. I was not yet married. In 1980, I was one of a group of four founding members of an organization that we called the Shabiba. The long-term goal of the Shabiba was to terminate the Israeli occupation of Palestinian land. We started educating the youth in the Gaza Strip about the evils of the Israeli occupation and organizing youths in cells and groups which could be activated to work against the occupation. The other three founding members and leaders of the organization were Abu Zafer, Muhammad Abu Mazcur, who later died of cancer, and Muhammad Dahlan. I became a leader of our youth movement at the age of nineteen.

The short-term goals of the Shabiba were educational. They were linked to the everyday life of the high school students or young workers in the Gaza Strip. We were quite successful. The idea of the Shabiba spread to the West Bank, and people there started setting up another branch of the organization. We were in constant communication with them. One of our initial major goals was to bring our young people to understand their situation of being oppressed and exploited by the Israelis; we wanted them to see clearly the situation in which they found themselves. A bit later, we also started working with university students.

Setting up a voluntary secret organization throughout the Gaza Strip was not a simple challenge. It required secretly setting up a committee of youths in every neighborhood. It required publishing secret declarations and a secret newsletter. How did we work?

At first there were three organizing cells of three members each. The first was in charge of educating and organizing the youth in the northern Gaza Strip, the second was in charge of the southern Gaza Strip. The third cell was in charge of organizing students of the Islamic University, which was the only university in the Gaza Strip. Each cell had three members. I was in charge of the northern cell. The cells started to organize new cells, slowly dividing the area so it would be covered and led by an organizing cell. After a few months we had five cells, then seven, then eleven. I was also active in organizing students from the Islamic University, hence many people, including teachers, thought that I was an enrolled student. My activities in the university concentrated on seeking out people who could lead cells of the Shabiba in different areas of the Gaza Strip and trying to enlist them into our ranks. These activities were successful.

Among the practical things that we wanted to teach members of the Shabiba was that when they work together, they have the power to change things. Thus, we organized groups of students to help farmers in the Gaza Strip harvest tomatoes and peas, to clean up the alleys in the refugee camps, and to help people who were building their houses. All work in the Shabiba was voluntary. We also organized youths to plant olive trees on land owned by Palestinians that the Israelis wanted to confiscate and give to Jewish settlers. We got young olive trees from a tree nursery near Tulcarem on the West Bank, which worked with us and secretly belonged to the Fatah. By planting trees, we wanted to show the Israelis, and the world, that Israeli forces were unjustly confiscating Palestinian land. Most of the land upon which we planted trees against confiscation was in the West Bank, but some of it was in the Gaza Strip. At times, albeit rarely, the planting of olive trees halted the confiscation of a small plot of land.

While we were setting up the Shabiba, we had almost no financial resources. Frequently, we leaders would contribute our own money to ensure that an activity would not be cancelled. After some months, a wealthy contractor in Gaza City let us use one of his offices. Lack of money at times led to drastic measures. I remember that we once suspended for six months our person who was in charge of finances, because he forgot where he had spent three dinars of our meager budget. Today three dinars is worth about four dollars. We cancelled the suspension after two months when he recalled to whom he had given the money. Now, when he meets me, he repeatedly says, "You suspended me for six months for a mistake about three dinars, while now some people who are in power in Palestine steal millions of dinars from our government budget and you sit quietly, doing nothing."

After a while, we organized women's cells in the Shabiba. At first hundreds, later thousands, of young women became involved in our activities. But women were not represented in the leadership of the entire movement. There were women leaders at the local level, who were independent and could make decisions about their areas and activities, but there were no women at the top leadership levels.

Only after three years, in 1983, did the Israelis become aware of some of our activities. You must remember that the Israelis had hundreds of Palestinian collaborators in the Gaza Strip working for them, but our activities were not comprehended for many months. I believe that one reason for our not being infiltrated by Israeli collaborators was that we leaders and activists in the Shabiba had no formal or regular meeting place. We would meet at random meeting places: in a cafe, at a home of a friend, or on a bench in a park.

In 1983, the Israelis began to create problems for us. I was not yet married and still lived with my parents, who knew nothing about my political activities.

There were internal problems in the Fatah as a result of the events of the 1982 Lebanon war. In December 1983, we decided to secretly organize a central demonstration in Jerusalem in support of Yasser Arafat. The activities of the Shabiba were in support of the Fatah, so it was natural for us to support Yasser Arafat. We felt that we had enough organized cells to plan a mass demonstration. For instance, in Jebalia Refugee Camp there were nine cells of the Shabiba, each of which could bring dozens, if not hundreds, of youths. There were also many Shabiba cells in the West Bank. I was a member of the joint organizing committee of leaders from the Gaza Strip and the West Bank, which planned and organized the demonstration. A large sum of money was smuggled to us from the leadership of the Palestine Liberation Organization (PLO) outside the Occupied Territories for expenses linked to the demonstration.

On December 13 and 14, 1983, the Shabiba brought thousands of Palestinian youths to the Al Aqsa Mosque in Jerusalem to demonstrate in support of Arafat. The youths came from all our centers of activity—from Jenin in the north of the West Bank to Rafah in the south of the Gaza Strip. After the prayer at the Al Aqsa Mosque we organized a demonstration and then paraded in the streets of Jerusalem shouting slogans supporting Arafat. You must remember that in that period, for most Jews, Arafat was their number one enemy, a man whom they vehemently hated. During the demonstration, there were many clashes with the Israeli police and border police. Many youths were arrested. The police used tear gas against us to disperse our parades and demonstrations. Fortunately, there were no deaths, but a few youths were wounded. For us, the demonstration was a major success. We had demonstrated, to ourselves and to the Israelis, the power of the Shabiba and its support for Arafat.

We decided to formally affiliate the Shabiba with the Fatah. Our declarations were in the name of the Fatah. Our contact in the exiled leadership of the Fatah was Abu Jihad. We had never met him, but we worked together. In 1983, I was appointed general coordinator for the Shabiba in the Gaza Strip. We used secret names so as to not disclose anything in case the Israelis caught our messages. For a period I was called "Lawi," then my name was changed and I was called "T," and then for a period my name was "Black." Our main way of corresponding with the leadership of the Fatah outside the Occupied Territories was by messages written on thin paper that people swallowed a short period before they crossed the border into Jordan.

This method was very reliable. We would fold the thin paper upon which the message was written very carefully, making it as small as possible. We would insert the paper into a very small tube made up of three layers of plastic; we would heat the plastic so it would melt and thus close the plastic tube with the message inside. The tube was very small and was not difficult to swallow. The messenger, who was traveling to Jordan, would be told to swallow the tube a few hours before reaching the border. After crossing the border, the messenger would find the small plastic tube in his or her excrement, remove the first two layers of plastic, and deposit the closed tube at an address that he or she had committed to memory. The messenger was told never to open the third layer, so that he or she would not know what was written in the message. From that address, the message was passed on to the leadership of the Fatah.

At times, the messenger, upon his or her return to Israel, would bring a reply that would pass the border in the same manner. Later, we also used this manner of conveying messages from our jailed leaders, who had been incarcerated by the Israeli authorities, to members of our organization who were active outside the jail. Most of the time the messengers to Jordan were elderly women, who knew that they were doing something important for our struggle for freedom of the Palestinian people and that the message was secret. Some of the messengers received payment. All of them acted responsibly; the messages reached their goals. Furthermore, there were no betrayals or mistakes. It never happened that messages conveyed in this manner were passed on to the Israeli authorities. This means of communication was our invention; it was not suggested by the leaders of the PLO in exile.

By 1984, the Shabiba was by far the largest youth organization in the Gaza Strip, dwarfing the youth organizations of the communists, of the people affiliated with George Habash, and of all other factions in the PLO. Although I still worked during the day in a small bookstore and lending library that I had acquired, I was very active in the Shabiba. The bookstore was a good place for my organizational work. I could receive messages, hidden in a book, and pass on messages, hidden in a book, to a supposed lender. Aside from this job, I would meet with the cell leaders from all the refugee camps and from Gaza City on a weekly basis. Thus, I worked daily in organizational and educational work.

I had to close the bookstore in order to get rid of the officers of the Israeli intelligence who began to observe my activities closely. These officers were stationed at Al-Wehda Street, and I still remember that one of them was called Abu Shareif and another Captain Dan. They would frequent my shop on their way to and from their offices. When I realized that I was being observed, I closed down the shop.

During 1984, every evening of the week I had meetings with Shabiba activists from various locations in the Gaza Strip. The meetings were always held in different places, which was also an organizational problem, since we did our best to avoid being discovered by Palestinian collaborators with Israel. When we met outside, say, in a park, we leaders would give instructions, and then all the people who had come to the meeting would disperse quickly. They would pass on the orders to other cells with whom they were in contact.

Despite our attempts to keep our activities secret, the Shabak soon learned that I had a leadership role in the Shabiba. They started trailing me. They would also arrest me before national occasions such as Land Day or Fatah Day. These were called precautionary arrests of supposed leaders of the youth organizations, and we were released after the national occasion had passed.

During that period, we also set up the structure of the joint organization of Shabiba groups in the West Bank and the Gaza Strip. After that, when they needed help in the West Bank, we would send them youths from the Gaza Strip to help. Although we now received some funds for our activities from the Palestinian organizations that were abroad, we were very strict about expenses and continued to report every shekel that we spent in the treasurer's report. Since my responsibilities were mainly organizational and educational, I was not involved in the day-to-day financial transactions. Hence, I don't remember the amount of our yearly budget or its breakdown into various items of expenses.

As our organization grew, a small group of activists decided to start military activities against the Israelis. This decision was in accordance with the instructions that we received from the Fatah leadership in exile. The group that initiated military activities was a minority. Most of the people affiliated with the Shabiba remained in the original organization and worked to continue enlarging, educating, and organizing the Shabiba. We decided that there would be a clear division between both groups of youths—they were two totally separate branches of the Fatah and the Shabiba. Thus, we who remained within the educational organization of the Shabiba knew nothing about the branch dedicated to military organization and military activities against the Israeli occupation.

In the middle of March 1985, I was arrested, interrogated, and tortured by the Israeli army. My watch was confiscated, and I was beaten and tied up in a very uncomfortable position for hours with a thick sack on my head so that I could hardly breathe. I was also subject to hot and cold showers. My interrogators from the Shabak were Abu Said, Abu Rabe, and Captain Jack. They interrogated me as to the nature of the Shabiba, and I repeatedly explained that it was a youth movement dedicated to social services. After eighteen days, I was released without being charged. My arrest was directly linked to the Shabiba activities at that time, particularly to our clashes with the Islamic Bloc at the Islamic University. I was arrested, supposedly as a precautionary measure, to halt the clashes. My arrest was also during the days that preceded Land Day, which falls at the end of March.

In March 1985, a verbal disagreement between activists of the Shabiba and Islamic fundamentalists at the Islamic University had turned violent. The direct reason for the disagreement was that our brothers from the Islamic Bloc at the university wanted to expel the Shabiba from all activity in the Islamic University. Our people refused to be expelled and violence erupted. The violence spilled into the streets and became quite wicked; it lasted for more than two weeks, with both sides using sticks, iron bars, and swords. There were quite a few youths wounded, some of whom had to be hospitalized. The Israelis were quite pleased with this development and did not interfere in the violent conflict.

In the early 1980s, the Israeli authorities were seeking an alternative to the widespread support for the PLO in the West Bank and the Gaza Strip. Probably, the broad international support for the PLO also worried them. To counter the PLO, the Israelis decided to support certain groups of Islamic fundamentalists in the Gaza Strip, including the Islamic Brothers. Hence, the Israeli authorities were pleased when the Islamic organizations at the Islamic University in Gaza became strong enough to challenge the Shabiba, which they knew was affiliated with the PLO. In addition, they were quite happy that violent disputes flared up between our different organizations in the Gaza Strip. They knew that these disputes weakened us as a nation that is struggling for freedom. During these two and a half weeks, Israeli army patrols often stood nearby, not interfering, while watching the violence between the members of the Shabiba and those of the Islamic Bloc.

After two and a half weeks of violent clashes, a group of mediators from the West Bank came to Gaza City to try to calm the situation. There were negotiation sessions and meetings of dialogue with leaders from both sides. Finally, both sides agreed not to use violence and to protect the students who were working for both organizations. But our brothers in the Islamic Bloc did not fulfill their side of the agreement, and quite rapidly they attained formal control of the university. They also wanted to totally silence our organization, but we adamantly refused. We continued to distribute leaflets and organize people to join the Shabiba.

Our activities led to renewed violence against us by our Islamic brothers. Our people then adopted a new tactic. When attacked by members of the Islamic Bloc, our men were told to go out into the street and throw rocks at the Israeli patrol cars that were always patrolling that area. This led to a clash in which the Israelis started firing at our men while the Islamic Bloc people were throwing rocks at them. We wanted to indicate by this action that our true enemies were the Israelis and that the Islamic Bloc was supporting the Israelis when they tried to limit our activities. My arrest, together with those of twenty other young men who were also arrested for precautionary reasons because many of them were active in the Shabiba, occurred during the struggle within the Islamic University. We were all released after eighteen days. The final result was that the Islamic movement controlled all political activity at the Islamic University.

After my release, I continued my organizational and educational activities in the Shabiba. But in August 1985, I was again arrested by the Israelis together with a few dozen young men, many of them leaders of the Shabiba. There were no military activities organized by the Shabiba at that time, and we were not charged with any wrongdoing. However, we were all sentenced to a year of administrative detention, which meant that we were incarcerated without a trial.

For the first few weeks we were jailed in Gaza Central Prison in Gaza City. While in prison we continued our organizational activities both in the prison and outside it, often by the messages that people who were released from prison swallowed before their release. After these weeks, we were transferred to a prison on the outskirts of Beer Sheva, inside Israel. From that prison, links with our people outside the prison were very difficult. While jailed in the prison at Beer Sheva, we had to work isolated from our people outside the prison, and we even felt isolated from the world. We decided to dedicate our time to our education.

For instance, while jailed in the prison near Beer Sheva, I took two courses in Hebrew language and two courses in English language. The teachers were fellow prisoners. The Hebrew that I now speak fluently was learned during my years in prison and not during the three years that I worked in Israel.

We were about 150 Palestinian prisoners in Beer Sheva prison. The prisoners belonged to different movements that struggled for Palestinian freedom, but the largest number of prisoners were members of the Shabiba. Our prison cell was large, nine meters long, and it housed seventy prisoners. There were seven toilets at the end of the room. Our life in prison was very well organized in order to further our struggle for freedom from Israeli occupation. We decided that each Palestinian prisoner had to participate every day in three obligatory learning sessions, each lasting at least one hour. The sessions were dedicated to his education and to the raising of his political and cultural awareness. In addition, we recommended that each prisoner dedicate two hours each day to reading and to personal study. Consequently, each prisoner had to spend at least five hours each day studying.

This atmosphere of joint study and discussion, of teaching each other and learning from each other, was most encouraging during the unjust incarceration. It was also encouraging to know what all the prisoners were studying—the syllabus of each course was distributed throughout the prison. At times, we had to convey the syllabus orally. Furthermore, the reality of learning something important every day spiritually enriched our struggle for freedom. All of us who spent time in prison benefited personally from this experience of learning together. Some people even stated that the best thing about the occupation was what was happening in the Israeli prisons.

When we had prisoners who were jailed for short periods, say a few months, we gave them intensive courses. They had to participate in five obligatory learning sessions each day. Quite frequently, we also examined the prisoners' comprehension of their readings. Each prisoner who finished one of the thirty books that were assigned in the general course was requested to give an oral report of what he had learned from the book. Afterwards, other prisoners questioned him and commented on the report.

In accordance with our organizational approach, while I was in jail my leadership role in the Shabiba had been taken over by someone else. We knew that at any moment a leader could be arrested, so we always appointed deputies to immediately replace the leader in case of arrest. This approach ensured the continual vitality of our movement.

After I was released from prison in the summer of 1986, I opened a sporting goods store in Omar Al Mukhtar Street near the central square in Gaza City. My attraction to sporting goods may have been a result of my long-term dedication to playing football. I was a member of the football team of the Gaza Sports Club, and we participated in football matches with other teams from the Gaza Strip and the West Bank. However, sports for me was always a hobby; my major dedication was to the struggle for Palestinian freedom.

Quite soon I passed the sporting goods store on to my brother, who changed it into a clothing store. I went to work full time at Hassan Al Weihaidi's international press office. In truth, I had been working part time in Hassan Al Wei-haidi's office since 1983. The reason was that we wanted information and sto-ries from the Shabiba and other organizations to reach a world audience. His press office had links with the international news agencies of Reuters and the Associated Press and had contacts with national news agencies in Rome, Paris, London, and New York. Hassan Al Weihaidi was very pleased to have people from the Shabiba work in his office. During 1986 and 1987 our work in his press office broadened; soon we were a large group of people who were gather-ing and sending abroad reports about our activities and the situation in the Gaza Strip. At times, such a report would be twenty to thirty pages long.

At first, we would transfer our reports by telephone. Later, our people in Paris sent us a facsimile machine, which had to be stored secretly, since Israeli army regulations dictated that we were not allowed to own fax machines. After the fax arrived, it was much easier to transfer information and to be in close contact with our people in Europe and the United States. A few times, the Israeli army sent soldiers to inspect Hassan Al Weihaidi's press office, but they found nothing. The army inspectors understood that we were a press office. In our office, they did not find anything that was not related to our press work. Needless to say, the infor-mation that we transmitted to press offices in the West Bank and abroad was dif-ferent from the information we sent to the exiled leadership of the Fatah.

After my release from jail in 1986, we decided that the entire organization of the Shabiba in the Gaza Strip would be led by a committee of three people. To-gether with Fares Hassona and Zakaria Al-Talmas, I served in this leadership committee. It was a joint leadership, with all three of us assuming leadership roles and accepting joint responsibility for our activities. We worked together amicably. When the opportunity arose it turned out that our organization, the Shabiba, was able to start and sustain a rebellion.

Official history says that the intifada broke out spontaneously on December 8, 1987, in response to an accident in which an Israeli truck driver, driving reck-lessly on a turn north of the Gaza Strip in Israel, hit a Palestinian car and killed four Palestinians and wounded seven others. Most of the casualties were from Jebalia Refugee Camp. When we heard of the accident, I had an idea that proved to be very successful. Two days previously an Israeli soldier had been stabbed and killed in the souk in Gaza City. I fabricated a story that the truck driver was a cousin of the slain Israeli soldier, and, in revenge, he had purposely killed the four Palestinians. I convinced my colleagues at Hassan Al Weihaidi's press of-fice that we must spread this false story to all news media and, of course, within the Gaza Strip, since it could bring people into the streets. They agreed. I sus-pected that spreading this false story might result in a demonstration or a se-ries of demonstrations of Palestinians against the Israeli occupation. In truth, this false story ignited the intifada. The grass-roots rebellion that began was beyond my wildest expectations.

It is important to emphasize that this grass-roots rebellion, the intifada, was very much based upon our organizational work in the Shabiba. We already had a working organization that was waiting to be used for freeing our people. We had nine youth committees in Jebalia Refugee Camp. On the evening of December 8, we told the leader of those nine committees, Suheil El Tuloli, that on the next day all high school students and all other youths should come to the funeral of the people from Jebalia who were killed in the truck accident and stage a mass demonstration against the Israelis. We also got the high school and the university students affiliated with us to join the demonstration. The demonstration was an overwhelming success. The number of participants and their ferocity totally surprised the Israeli army. They used live ammunition to shoot at the demonstrators who attacked the army camp in Jebalia with rocks; one of our youth leaders, who was a member of our administrative board of the Shabiba, was killed, and many other youths were wounded.

That evening the rebellion spread to Gaza City. Due to the unprecedented number of youths hit by the Israeli bullets, there was not enough blood for transfusions for all of the wounded who needed them. We, the leaders of the Shabiba, visited the wounded, who had all been sent to Shiffa Hospital in Gaza City. When we learned of the need for blood for transfusions, we decided to ask the students of the Islamic University to donate blood for the wounded. When we arrived at the campus, we perceived that the Islamic University students had joined the rebellion. Students from the university were busy throwing rocks at the Israeli cars that patrolled that frequently used street; they were engaging the Israelis in street battles. The battles were so fierce and prolonged that the administration of the Islamic University decided to suspend all classes. They gave two reasons for this decision to close the university until, supposedly, matters quieted down. First, they did not want to give the Israeli soldiers a reason to enter the campus. Second, the university was for education only.

In response to our appeal, many students of the Islamic University came to donate blood. In the meantime, in Shatti Refugee Camp, which adjoins Gaza City, a large demonstration against the Israeli occupation had been organized by different Palestinian factions. The demonstration marched toward Shiffa Hospital throwing rocks at Israeli soldiers. Again the Israelis fired live ammunition, and one youth was killed and others wounded. The slain youth became our second martyr on that day. On the morrow, a general strike was called in the entire Gaza Strip. The strike was successful. Stores were closed; people did not go to work.

Coordination between our people was very difficult. We sensed, however, that with the expressions of outrage by our youths, a new period was beginning and that we must work rapidly so as to partially direct the events. The first evening we held a meeting of the leaders of all factions of the Palestinian people and decided to work together. The factions set up a joint leadership council of four people. In that council, I represented the Fatah, Marwan Al Kafarma represented the People's Front for the Liberation of Palestine (PFLP), Tawfik Al Mabhouh represented the Communist Party, and Jamal Zakoot represented the Democratic Front for the Liberation of Palestine (DFLP). We immediately started to issue written statements, encouraging people to continue the demonstrations and the deeds that express our rejection of the Israeli occupation; the statements were signed by the United Leadership of the Intifada, without specifying names. Our written statements were distributed throughout the Gaza Strip.

The next day our people in Gaza City continued the demonstrations and the throwing of rocks at Israeli patrols and cars. Clashes erupted again and again. On the third day the demonstrations and the throwing of rocks at Israeli soldiers spread to the Middle Area of the Gaza Strip. After a few days, the rebellion of Palestinian youths had spread to the West Bank and included all of the areas of Palestine occupied by Israel.

Looking back, I can now say that within those first days, the intifada had reached the point of no return. At first, we wanted it to continue until January 1, 1988, which was the anniversary of the establishment of the Fatah. Fearing that the intifada would ruin our people economically, on January 1, 1988, we issued a statement advising our people not to stop working in Israel as day laborers. But the intifada continued for years after January 1, 1988. People, and especially our young men, did not want to give up the struggle. Hence, they repeatedly attacked Israeli soldiers with rocks, closed roads with burning tires, wrote anti-Israeli graffiti along all the streets, and refused to give up the daily struggle for freedom.

The intifada surprised the exiled leadership of the PLO, who resided outside the occupied territories. During the first month of the intifada, the outside leaders were merely recipients of information. By telephone and fax we were in almost daily contact with Abu Jihad, who was commander of all activities against Israel and was later killed by Israeli commandos during a raid in Tunis. Abu Jihad agreed that we leaders on the ground must make the decisions, since we were on the spot and could perceive the developments. As the struggle continued, Abu Jihad left the organization and the daily decisions to the local leadership in the Occupied Territories. That was a wise decision. After he was killed, those who took his place in the exiled leadership tried to intervene in our decisions. My impression was that this external intervention in our day-to-day decisions had a negative effect on our struggle. There also was no funding from the leadership outside the Occupied Territories. From the beginning, our understanding was that the main role of the exiled leadership was to utilize the intifada for political gains and for media coverage of the injustice of the Israeli occupation.

On February 28, 1988, at 2:00 A.M., the Israelis broke into my house, conducted a search, and arrested me. For quite a while, I had known that soon they would probably arrest me, since a few days earlier other leading members of our joint leadership had been arrested. During that round of arrests, the Israelis also discovered the printing press in Abu Dis near Jerusalem, where we had printed all our leaflets. Unfortunately, the army unit that arrested me also confiscated the facsimile in my house, which I had been using up to half an hour before my arrest.

When I arrived at Gaza Central Prison, the Israeli soldiers took me to change clothes and then to investigation. But before taking me to change clothes, they took me to a cold shower, gave me a piece of soap, and did not let me out of the cold water until I had used up the soap. It was a cold winter night and the water was freezing. If I tried to get out from under the freezing water the Israeli soldiers would beat me or kick me, forcing me back under the shower. Later, I learned that some of my comrades had eaten their bars of soap so as to get out of the freezing water. I rubbed the piece of soap on the wall until it disappeared. The ordeal took close to half an hour.

After I was dressed in prison garb, I was taken to investigation, which meant being beaten and tortured. The Israeli investigators, who knew Arabic fluently, had many ways of insulting, beating, and torturing us Palestinians during the many days of interrogating us. For instance, they would tie me, standing, to the wall and cover my head with a stinking sack and let me remain there for hours before calling me for questioning. Or they would tie me to a small chair on which I was forced to sit for hours, again with my head covered by a stinking sack, before calling me for questioning. When I was finally called in to the questioning room, there would be at least three interrogators. They would ask me questions while I was tied and beat me when I didn't answer. They would spit in my face and trip me to the floor and put their foot on my head. All of their questions were concentrated around one topic: Who is responsible for the intifada? Why does it continue?

Finally, I was put on trial for organizing activities against the Israeli regime and sentenced to three years in prison. I spent most of the three years in the large Ketziot Prison Camp, situated in the desert in Israel, together with thousands of other Palestinian prisoners. This period in prison was similar to the period I spent in Beer Sheva prison. We prisoners organized our daily life around studying and education, so as to be able to further our struggle for freedom. I was released from prison in 1991 and returned to my leadership role in the Shabiba.

I was in a leadership position in the Shabiba until close to the arrival of Yasser Arafat in the Gaza Strip on July 1, 1994. A few months before that date, we activists in the leadership positions began to feel that the ways by which the Palestinian Authority in the Gaza Strip was being established were quite mistaken. Many of us sensed that we were going to be dismissed and other people, who had not participated actively in the intifada, now would be leaders. We were convinced that Abu Ammar was not putting the right people in the right places. Such decisions greatly peeved us. There were no correct procedures in appointing people to positions in the Palestinian Authority. We also felt that the Fatah movement, as the mother of the struggle for Palestinian freedom and independence, should serve as an enlightening example for others. We were very disillusioned when we discovered that the Fatah provided no such example in relation to appointments of people to positions of power or in establishing procedures for putting the right man in the right place. One result of our disillusionment was that I did not participate in the celebrations when Yasser Arafat arrived in Gaza on July 1, 1994.

On July 2, 1994, at 11:30 P.M., Arafat convened a meeting with us, the leaders of the intifada, whom he called "the rebels." The meeting took place at the Palestine Hotel in Gaza City. The meeting lasted until 5:30 A.M. the following day. We explained to Abu Ammar our reservations about public issues. We also felt that some of the people who had been appointed to important positions had had much too cordial relations with the Israelis. Although Arafat dissolved the tension at the end of the meeting by asking us to always be close to him, we felt betrayed. I returned to work in journalism and no longer sought a position in the Palestinian Authority. Other members of our group of leaders were so dissatisfied that they decided to emigrate from the Gaza Strip. I still feel that I should stay here in the Gaza Strip and continue to struggle for a worthy Palestinian State. I am still in contact with many of the leaders of the Shabiba.

In general, we support the Palestinian Authority and its struggle for a Palestinian State. Our grass-roots involvement is very significant, and can be a great assistance to Abu Ammar. He recognizes that fact. In various incidents, when the Hamas tried to undermine the support of the Palestinian Authority, we gave the Authority much help. Through our many activities, we succeeded in convincing the people that the Hamas approach is dangerous for our national goals.

I am not very optimistic about the future. I believe that even a peace agreement will bring only a temporary stop to the aggression between Israelis and Palestinians. Many Palestinians still want the land from which their forefathers were expelled in 1948. The peace agreement will be about the borders of 1967. I do not believe that the people will give up their wish to return to the land, and this will probably bring renewed violence even after there is a Palestinian State. I suspect that the peace agreement will merely be a temporary armistice.

Chapter 5

Nehad Mansour

I was born on December 11, 1970, in Jebalia Refugee Camp. I have five brothers and three sisters, all older than I. Both my parents have died. In 1948, my parents fled to the refugee camp from East Bitan near Kastina, in the center of the Negev in Palestine and what is now Israel.

After 1967, my father worked for many years in Israel, mainly as a construction worker. My eldest brother, who is around fifty-two years old, was a teacher who worked in Libya for many years. In 1992 he resigned his teaching job in Libya and returned to the Gaza Strip. My second eldest brother also worked in Libya as a teacher. He resigned his job in 1994 and returned to the Gaza Strip where he is now working at an institution for the handicapped. After completing high school, both brothers received scholarships to study in Egypt. After graduating in Egypt, they went to Libya where they obtained better-paying jobs than in the Gaza Strip. While they were studying, they received financial support for living expenses from my father. Later, when they got jobs, they regularly sent us small amounts of money which helped us put up with the harsh economic conditions prevailing in the Gaza Strip.

My third brother did not complete secondary school and worked as a laborer in Israel. Later he became a merchant who sold goods to Israel. He has a magnetic identification card issued by the Israeli military. That card allows him to enter Israel. My fourth brother also has a magnetic card and works as a construction worker in Israel, where salaries are much higher than in the Gaza Strip; my fifth brother has a blacksmith's shop in Gaza City. During the intifada, two of my brothers were jailed for months, under the administrative detention decree. But being jailed during the intifada was not something out of the ordinary. My mother and sisters did not work.

The house in which I grew up in Jebalia Refugee Camp was very small, around seventy square meters. That was the standard size allotted to a refugee family. The roof was made of asbestos and tin sheets, and when the winter rain-storms arrived, it leaked. During the hot days of the summer the roof would heat the house, making it unbearable to sit inside. A few times, when the winds were especially strong and nasty, a few of the tin sheets were blown off the roof. When the wind calmed, we would have to search for them, and my father and elder brothers would fix the tin sheets back onto the roof. Our house had two small bedrooms, a narrow living room, a kitchen, and a bathroom. At first, my parents slept with the small children in one room, and the older brothers slept in another room. Later, when we grew older, some of us slept in the living room.

As children, we despised staying in the overcrowded house of Jebalia Refugee Camp, where there was no place to move about or play. We would spend most of the time outside, playing in the narrow alleys of the refugee camp. The alleys of Jebalia were not paved; they were dusty and full of garbage. Many of the ad-joining houses had no gaps between them. After it rained, the dust in the alleys became a sticky mud with many dirty puddles filled with garbage. But these narrow alleys were the only place where we children could play. We had no playgrounds. In the entire camp, there was not even one small garden with a green lawn or some plants. Like almost all the children in the refugee camp, we wore simple clothes and plastic shoes.

When I was young, there were maybe two televison sets in our quarter of the camp, in the houses of families who could afford them. At times, we children would congregate in one of these houses to watch TV. I especially liked to watch films about children in Israel or in Jordan, who could play games and romp in playgrounds. We knew and saw that they enjoyed much better living condi-tions than we had in the refugee camp, and we hoped that one day we would be able to play like them with real toys and real sports equipment. We played with balls and other toys that we made from the trash that was dumped in the streets. Around 1982, when I was twelve years old, our family finally bought a television set.

Playing with trash, I remember, caused many diseases and rashes. I had an additional brother and sister who died of measles. At that time, among the Palestinians in the refugee camps there was not much awareness of how to deal with such sicknesses; also, there was almost no awareness of the need to pre-vent infections and diseases. During my childhood, there was very little medi-cal care given at the UNWRA clinic in the camp. The doctors and nurses who worked at the clinic had a very rudimentary knowledge of health care, and there was very little hospital care that was available to the refugees in the Gaza Strip.

As refugees, every month we received flour, cooking oil, sugar, and some tins of food from UNWRA. But, during my early childhood the food allotment was not sufficient. After two weeks or, at most, eighteen days, all the UNWRA food would be eaten. We would be hungry for two weeks, until the beginning of the next month and the new distribution of food. During each month's twelve-day period of hunger, we would purchase whatever food we could with the money that my father and brothers had earned. We would eat only one meal a day since their salaries were very low. Another aspect of our poverty was that until I was nine years old we would heat everything, including our food, on wood that we gathered in nearby orchards and from leftover wood in the streets. Even the water to wash ourselves was wood heated. When I was nine, my father brought home a kerosene stove that he had bought in Israel, and we were delighted.

At first, I was a pupil in the Faluja primary school in Jebalia Refugee Camp; after that I studied for three years in Jaffa School, the UNRWA secondary school in Gaza City. I completed eleven grades of education and after being wounded I studied a bit at business school in Bir Zeit but did not complete my studies. In primary and secondary school, I liked to read Arab literature and especially Arab poetry. I also spent much time playing basketball during my years at school.

I joined the popular committee of the Shabiba, the youth, in Jabalia soon after the intifada began in December 1987. (Shabab in Arabic means young men, ranging from sixteen to thirty-five years old.) We were between twenty and thirty pupils in the committee, which numbered around seventy. We had no knowledge as to who were the higher leaders of the Shabiba; we only knew who was our direct leader. We agreed that such secrecy was necessary for the success of the Palestinian struggle. We also recognized that if we were arrested by the Israeli forces and subjected to torture, it would be best to know as little as possible. Later I learned that there were designated hiding places where higher leaders would leave messages to their group leaders. All this was done in order to ensure secrecy and limit knowledge of the participants as to the structure of the Shabiba. Due to this method, there were instances when a top leader of the Shabiba fled abroad before being arrested by the Israelis; evidently, the leader feared that under torture he might disclose the entire system of the Shabiba and the places where messages were hidden.

Our role in the Jebalia committee was to organize youths and pass orders to other members of the Shabiba, telling them how to participate in the intifada. We would organize our peers to throw stones at Israeli soldiers, write anti-Israeli graffiti on the walls, and beat up drug dealers and people who sold and consumed alcoholic beverages. Our assumption was that drug dealers were Palestinian collaborators, who provided information to the Israeli authorities; in return the Israeli authorities gave them drugs to sell. According to our understanding, the orders we received came from the PLO in Tunis. The only person we knew in the hierarchy of the command was our direct commander, who brought us the orders that we believed came from Tunis. We understood that he was the intifada commander of Jebalia Refugee Camp.

One of our roles as members of the popular committee of the Shabiba in Jebalia was to investigate local collaborators with Israel. If they were not collaborators who had been involved in killing Palestinians, we would attempt to bring them to confess their mistakes, repent, and change their ways—which meant that they must immediately stop collaborating with Israel. If they were stubborn and continued to collaborate, even after being warned repeatedly, we would be much more demanding; we were especially harsh with collaborators who had participated in killing Palestinians. In such instances, we would force the collaborators to confess, videotape the confession, and then have them punished by the punitive forces of the intifada. We, the members of the popular committee, did not participate in the acts of punishment. That was the role of the punitive forces, who were also called the striking forces. They would physically punish the collaborator. At times, they would have the collaborator put to death.

Jebalia Refugee Camp, which housed around 80,000 Palestinians, was divided into thirteen blocks. During the intifada, each block was policed by a popular committee of the Shabiba; this same committee also organized the daily activities of the intifada against Israel by leading the youth and the other residents in the acts of rebellion. Thus each area of the camp had its own specific popular committee which both led in the rebellion and policed the area. The punitive forces of Jebalia were not attached to a specific block; they helped all the popular committees.

The popular committee to which I belonged was in charge of a block that numbered around 6,000 people. We investigated around forty collaborators, and quite often we succeeded in having them change their ways. I should add that at times we failed, and some of the people we investigated still collaborate with the Israeli forces today. In addition to leading the intifada, policing, and investigating collaborators, we were also, at times, in charge of distributing contributions of food to the population of the camp. I remember that a few times we organized a distribution of sacks of flour to the residents of Jebalia.

On the day I was wounded, March 18, 1989, I had studied in the morning at Jaffa Secondary School in Gaza City. As I was walking back to my home in Jebalia Camp, I saw groups of people gathering to protest. I hurried to my house, left my school kit at home, and joined one of the gatherings. All the groups were protesting the killings of two Palestinian children by Israeli military forces. We started throwing rocks at an Israeli patrol of eight soldiers in a vehicle. The soldiers wore green berets, but not the green berets of the border police. They started to attack us and as I turned to run from them, I was shot with a live bullet in the lower back. That shot, I later learned, paralyzed me from my waist down. I fell.

Some of my comrades picked me up and tried to carry me away from the area of the shooting. But the shooting continued and they were afraid, so they lay me down and fled. Some Israeli soldiers from the patrol approached, saw me lying on the ground, and started to beat me with their rifles. They beat me in the back where I had been wounded, and also in my knees. An UNRWA ambulance arrived in order to take me to a hospital. But the soldiers did not allow the ambulance to approach me. They forced the ambulance driver to drive away. A few moments later my comrades from the Shabiba again started throwing rocks at the soldiers. The soldiers returned to their vehicle to respond to the rock throwers. They left me on the ground, and the UNRWA ambulance, which had been waiting nearby, utilized the opportunity to come and pick me up.

When I was shot I was fully conscious. I did not feel the lower part of my body, but I did feel pains in my back and my spine. When the Israeli soldiers surrounded me, I was sure that my end had arrived and that they would beat me to death. I was so exhausted that I made no attempt to stop them. I did scream when they beat me. I screamed and screamed because I thought that they were going to kill me.

The ambulance that finally picked me up took me to an UNRWA infirmary in Jebalia Refugee Camp. There I received first aid. From there I was sent to El Ahli Hospital in Gaza City, where I was X-rayed. From there I was transferred to an orthopedic department in Nasser Hospital in Khan Yunis, where I was operated upon and the bullet removed from my spine. I spent ten days in the hospital in Khan Yunis and from there was transferred to El Mukassed Hospital in Jerusalem where I spent two months recuperating. I returned to the Gaza Strip, and it took quite a while until the Israeli army allowed me to go to Jordan for additional treatment.

At first, the so-called civil authorities of the Israeli army refused to give me permission to travel to Jordan. Only after the U.N. representatives and workers from the International Red Cross intervened on my behalf with the Israeli authorities was the permission granted. The Jordanian doctors at the Hussein Medical City in Jordan told me that there was no hope for restoring my spinal cord. That was when I finally accepted the fact that I would not walk again. Indeed, the Jordanian doctors were right. My being paralyzed from the waist down is final. I was sent for consultations with doctors in Russia, Britain, and the United States. All the doctors said that my condition of being confined to a wheelchair is final.

My mother had died in 1984 and my father was ill on the day that I was shot; he was unable to walk. After the incident in which I was wounded, a curfew was declared in Jebalia, so friends and family could not come to visit me in the hospital. When the curfew was removed a few days later, people started to visit me, mainly my friends from the Shabiba. Unfortunately, the treatment at the hospitals in Gaza was not very good. One of the reasons for poor treatment was that the hospitals lacked equipment. In El Mukassed Hospital in Jerusalem the treatment was better.

I am not angry at what was done to me. I'll be angry and sorry if there will not be a just and lasting peace with Israel. We, as Palestinians, open our hands for peace, but the other side, Israel, does not show interest in peace. Suffering in the Gaza Strip continues, and Israel procrastinates and does not fulfill its major obligations as defined in the Oslo Agreement.

I am not sorry that I joined my schoolfriends from the Shabiba and became a member of the Shabiba committee in Jebalia Refugee Camp. I am proud that

I actively participated in the intifada. When we joined the intifada, we knew that we might be shot or jailed or killed; but we felt that it was the right thing to do—for our integrity and our country and our people. I was not the first or the last Palestinian to be wounded; thousands were wounded in the daily clashes with the armed forces of the Israeli oppressor. I was paralyzed from the waist down, but I was willing to give my life for my people. Now I am a supporter of the peace with Israel. As I fought for the freedom of my people, I now want to fight for peace. I feel no need for personal revenge. I feel great sympathy for Israelis who were wounded during the intifada, including those who became handicapped like me.

I was married exactly five years after the day I was wounded, on March 18, 1994. I met my wife, Sabah, through the activities I had undertaken with others to establish the Society for the Handicapped of the Intifada in the Gaza Strip. Sabah had been studying journalism at the YMCA in Gaza City, and that was the place our society would meet. Together with other women, Sabah supported the handicapped and our society. Sabah has a slight limp from birth. We got to know each other and spent some time together at the meetings of our society at the YMCA. After four or five months we decided to get married. Her family, however, at first refused the match; I suspect they refused because I am handicapped. They reside in the Sheikh Radwan area of Gaza City.

Mainly the older people in Sabah's family were against our getting married. The younger people supported us, and finally, after a few months, the younger people prevailed. They said that my being paralyzed was a result of my participation in the Palestinian fight for freedom, hence I was worthy of any Palestinian woman. Consequently, they continued, it was wrong to refuse to allow Sabah to marry me. The elderly members of the family were afraid that she would have to support me and also care for me. They thought that I would not be able to purchase a home for us or have a family. But slowly they understood that it was different with me, and they finally agreed to the marriage. They now see that I have an apartment with good furniture in it, and also three daughters, and a car. My wife and I earn enough to support our family.

On my wedding day, Israeli soldiers killed a Palestinian here in the Gaza Strip, and a curfew was declared in Gaza City. It also was not many days after Baruch Goldstein had massacred twenty-nine Palestinians in the Ibrahimi Mosque at the Tomb of the Patriarchs in Hebron. So we decided not to have a large, open wedding, just a modest, small wedding for our family and close friends.

Since I had been severely wounded without in any way threatening the lives of Israeli soldiers, I went to court against the Israeli army and demanded reparations. We settled out of court after seven years and I received 120,000 shekels, about $40,000, but my lawyers took 25 percent of that sum. The sum that remained helped me to purchase the small apartment where I now live with my wife and daughters. It is in an apartment building built by the European Housing Council, and it is for people who are social and humanitarian cases. I was eligible, and had to pay $8,000 to the bank to get the apartment. In addition, I agreed to pay $100 a month for twenty-five years. Living in the apartment makes it easier for me, since it is easier for me to go to the bathroom and to take a shower.

In 1992, UNRWA gave me $11,000, which I used to open a shoe store in Gaza, from which I could make a living. The store did well and for a short period I could help my family financially. But I did not continue in that work and no longer have the shoe store. I sold it after getting involved in founding the Society for the Handicapped in the Gaza Strip. I was one of the founders of the Society for the Handicapped, and establishing it interested me much more than selling shoes. After a while, I understood that my involvement in the Society for the Handicapped was ruining my store, since I was not available to sell shoes many hours of the day. Four years after it had opened, I sold the store at about a 60 percent loss.

Today there are 5,600 members registered in the Society for the Handicapped in the Gaza Strip. I firmly believe that establishing the society was a worthy undertaking, and I am not sorry to have given up my shoe store. Today I receive a salary from Force 17, the force that guards President Yasser Arafat. But, I do not work for the force. I work as a volunteer at the Palestinian Society for the Handicapped in the Gaza Strip, and get my salary from Force 17. I receive 1,400 shekels a month ($350). My wife also works at the central headquarters of Force 17. She is a lieutenant and receives a monthly salary of 1,600 shekels ($400).

The Society for the Handicapped in the Gaza Strip endeavors to help the handicapped in three areas: treatment, rehabilitation, and work opportunities. We recognize that the situation in all three of these areas is very difficult, even in the parts of the homeland governed by the Palestinian Authority. Many of the handicapped receive minimal help from the authorities. The medical treatment is often miserable, and the department of labor has not helped them much in finding jobs. But we are endeavoring to change that situation, even though until now we have only been able to help in, at most, 15 percent of the instances where we intervened. Usually a handicapped person receives only 150 shekels ($38) a month as living allowance, which is definitely not enough. I would say that it is enough for a family of four to live on for four days.

I became affiliated with Force 17 as a result of Yasser Arafat's meeting with the leaders of the Society for the Handicapped in the Gaza Strip. Arafat came to the Gaza Strip, to the land of Palestine, on July 1, 1994. I was among the wounded of the intifada who formally greeted him on July 2, 1994. In September of that year we, 360 of the severely handicapped of the intifada, asked to meet Arafat again, so as to ask for a monthly allowance. He decided to enlist us in Force 17. Our salary is the only allowance we receive from the Palestinian government. At times, I make a little extra money as a dealer in used cars. I have army health insurance and receive medical aid from the army.

Quite soon after being wounded, I decided to organize a men's basketball team of Palestinian handicapped. I was in charge of sport in the Society for the

Handicapped in the Gaza Strip. At first only a few people joined the team, but soon we had some good players, many of whom I chose and convinced to join the team. I was elected captain of the team. At first, we received support from merchants, but now we receive support from the Ministry of Youth and Sport of the Palestinian Authority. We can also apply directly to Arafat, who gave us $17,000 to fly to Atlanta in 1996 to participate in the world basketball games for handicapped people. I usually practice basketball three hours each day with the entire team. I have a special wheelchair for playing basketball. We play on the regular basketball court. Today there are four handicapped men's basketball teams in the Gaza Strip and seven handicapped men's basketball teams in the West Bank.

The Ministry of Youth and Sport decides who will represent Palestine in international matches. I was nominated by the Sport Union in the Gaza Strip and the West Bank to be responsible for the handicapped basketball team. I chose three players from the Gaza Strip and seven from the West Bank, and together they are the team that represents Palestine in international games. Most of the team members were wounded during the intifada and many also receive a salary from Force 17. We played in a tournament in Jordan against teams from Lebanon, Syria, Jordan, and Egypt.

I want a lasting peace with Israel, but right now the Israelis are oppressing us both economically and in their harsh military decisions that deny us freedom of movement. They are procrastinating in fulfilling their responsibilities, especially in implementing the peace agreements that they signed in Oslo and afterward. Despite our many years of struggle during the intifada and the many sacrifices that we made, in many crucial respects the Israeli military occupation has not ended. Major examples of this occupation are the many Jewish settlements and the ongoing presence of the Israeli army on our land. Israel still controls much of the best land in the Gaza Strip.

As a person who was wounded in our struggle for freedom, I want a just peace, which means the establishment of an independent Palestinian State beside the State of Israel.

Chapter 6

Nema El Helo

I was born a healthy female child in 1952 in the town Jebalia, in a small house given to my father and mother for six years by a family who recognized their sad plight. My extended family had fled to the Gaza Strip during the 1948 War from the area of Bet Jerja, a village close to Majdal, which is now in the area of the Israeli city Ashkelon. In 1953, my family moved to Jebalia Refugee Camp which is adjacent to the town Jebalia.

In the camp, UNRWA gave my family a two-room house with a small kitchen. In that house my parents and we children, together six people, slept in one room, and my grandparents and uncle slept in another room. Later my father bought a small house for our family. It was in Jebalia Refugee Camp not far from our former house. My childhood and youth were spent in Jebalia Refugee Camp.

I was my parents' third child, among those who lived. An elder sister had died early in her life. My mother said that this elder sister, who was her first child, had died probably because of the difficult conditions that the family lived through during the flight from Bet Jerja to the Gaza Strip. Before my parents fled from Bet Jerja to the Gaza Strip, my father, who was the eldest of two sons, was a farmer; he farmed our family land together with my grandfather. In the area of Bet Jerja, our family had many dunams of land on which they raised crops. They also had a citrus grove which yielded oranges and lemons, and there was a small vineyard for grapes. My grandfather would often share his memories of life at Bet Jerja, on the land that had belonged to our family.

In the early 1970s, after the Gaza Strip had been occupied by Israeli military forces in the 1967 war and we Palestinians could drive to Israel, my grandfather decided that he wanted to see his land again. Our extended family that lived in the Gaza Strip joined him. We hired two cars, took with us some food and water, and drove to our land. My grandfather wanted to show the family land to all

members of his family. When we found our family land, we discovered that
there were Jews living on it and tilling it. My grandfather wept when he saw
the big house in which he had lived. He showed us a well near the house. I also
wept when I was told that this land belonged to our family.

The Jews who were living on the land were disturbed by our walking around
what they considered to be their property. A quarrel erupted, and one of the
Jews even shot into the air. An Israeli man intervened and quieted the quarrel;
but that peacemaking Israeli told us clearly that he would not intervene in this
matter again. I should add that in our family there was a general feeling, the
major source of which was the beliefs and thinking of my father and grandfather, that we should struggle continually so as to return to our land. That is
one reason, probably, that my father and grandfather often visited our land in
Israel and walked around it—when such visits were still permitted.

After my family arrived in the Gaza Strip in 1948, my father had no work
and for many months the family lived as refugees, supported solely by
UNRWA and by help from others. After a few years, my father was trained to
drive a truck, and he worked for quite a few years as a truck driver in the Gaza
Strip. In the early 1960s, my father traveled to Egypt and worked for some
years on the High Dam that the Egyptians were building at Aswan.

As children of refugees, we received a free meal at 10:00 A.M. every day at an
UNRWA food distribution center in Jebalia Refugee Camp. We would wait in
long lines to receive our daily meal at that food center. I remember that there
were times when we would wait in line for an hour and a half in order to receive that meal. My mother would not feed us before the UNRWA meal, so
that we would be hungry and eat what was distributed to us. I believe that most
mothers in Jebalia Refugee Camp did the same.

The daily meal that we received usually consisted of a plate of rice with small
pieces of meat, and a glass of milk. The food distribution center also distributed
milk for the young children early in the morning, at 6:30. Every day my
mother or grandmother would awake early and go to the food center to stand
in line in order to receive milk for us. At times, the food distribution center
would distribute fruit and eggs to refugee families. One of our neighbors had
advance information about such food distribution, and she always told my
mother to go get the allotted fruit and eggs for us.

One of my chores as a six-year-old child was to help my mother gather wood
for our cooking oven, which was made of clay. We would search for and gather
wood in the scrub and the tree groves that were about an hour's walking distance from Jebalia Refugee Camp. When we finished gathering the wood, my
mother would put a small sack of wood on my head and a large sack of wood on
her head, and together we would walk the hour distance to our home. If my
sack fell off my head, I would be beaten. We cooked on wood because, usually,
we did not have money to buy fuel for a kerosene stove; many years passed
until we could afford a gas stove. During my childhood, in Jebalia Refugee
Camp there were no gas stoves.

I commenced my schooling at an UNRWA elementary school in the refugee camp. My family had difficulty finding the money to get me a blue and white school uniform and the required leather bag for my schoolbooks. I have few memories of my school life, and these memories are linked to physical activities. I was not interested in learning subjects such as history or geography. I loved physical education, scouting, and sports. I was especially attracted to basketball and jumping, and I dedicated many hours to these sports. Perhaps the reason I was quite good in sports had to do with the fact that, since childhood, I had been accustomed to hard work, such as carrying water and wood on my head for long distances. I remained in school until I finished the ninth grade.

I clearly remember some incidents that occurred during the 1967 war between Israel and Egypt. My grandfather had planted orange and lemon trees near our house, and not far from the trees there was a deep ditch in which one could crouch or sit. We all entered the ditch and stayed there when there was shelling. Once after some shelling I went to a neighbor's house and saw a woman who had been killed while playing with her nine-month-old baby; the child was still alive, sitting on the mother's chest. I wept when I saw this scene. The woman's name was Miasar and she was very beautiful. I believe that such scenes led me to believe that we must fight to recover our land and that we must seek revenge for our suffering at the hands of the Jewish people and the Israeli army.

In 1967, we still believed that we would return to our land. People did not want to build their own houses in or near Jebalia Refugee Camp because they all wanted to return to their villages and towns in Israel. UNRWA officials seemed to agree with our longing to return to our land. They did not encourage us to build better houses to replace the flimsy refugee shacks that they had given us. Only in the 1980s did families in our refugee camp begin to build better, more spacious houses.

One of my first acts in fighting against the Israeli occupation of the Gaza Strip occurred near our house a few months after the June 1967 war, when I was fifteen years old. On that day, by chance, I met a Palestinian man with a rifle. He was trying to evade being detected by the Israeli armed forces. He also was afraid of passing their army checkpoints with a rifle. He asked me to check if there were Israeli soldiers in the vicinity while he concealed himself in our yard. I checked and told him that there were soldiers in the area. I suggested that he let me hide the rifle for him and that he escape from the area. I told him our name and address so that he could retrieve the rifle when he was ready. He told me that he was from the nearby village, Bet Lahia. He gave me the rifle and vanished. I took the rifle and asked our neighbor to hide it in the roof of her house until the Palestinian freedom fighter would come to retrieve it. She hid it. A few hours later, soldiers from the Israeli army searched our houses, but they did not find the rifle.

Three months later the freedom fighter returned and found me at home, and we gave him the rifle. But to make sure that he would be able to bring the rifle safely to his house, we concealed it in a sack; I carried the sack and walked with him to his destination. He was very pleased with me; he said that he wanted to teach me to use arms against our Israeli oppressors.

I have additional memories from my teenage years that are linked to the Israeli oppression. There were men in Jebalia Refugee Camp who were active in the resistance to the Israeli occupation, and we knew about them. On one occasion when a few of these men were together, a bomb exploded and one of my cousins was killed. The Israelis were not responsible for the explosion, which was probably an accident. But my family's and my anger at his death, at the funeral and during the period of mourning, was directed toward the Israeli oppressors.

In the late fall of 1970—I remember that it was after President Jamal Abd-El Nasser's death—a woman suddenly came to one of my woman cousins, Ghalia, who had links to the Palestinian resistance. I was with Ghalia when that woman, who was not from Jebalia Refugee Camp, approached her with a sad message. She told us that there were two wounded Palestinian freedom fighters hiding in an orchard not far from our camp. I was acquainted with that area of orchards. She said that the Israelis were searching for the freedom fighters and wanted to arrest them. She stressed that the wounded men needed help, especially a doctor who would tend their wounds. That day Ghalia was involved in other activities, and I volunteered to assist the wounded warriors. I learned from the woman where the freedom fighters were hiding; I told her where to wait for me not far from that place while I went to find medical assistance.

I knew a doctor named Dr. Rashad who was a patriot and worked at a hospital. I went to a nurse with whom I was acquainted and who worked with Dr. Rashad. I asked her to come with me and bring some medicine for our wounded freedom fighters. The nurse refused to go with me. She said that one of the reasons for her refusal was that she knew the identity of the wounded fighters and did not support their political approach. I argued with her that the identity of the fighters was not relevant, since they needed medical assistance.

While I was arguing with the nurse, Dr. Rashad entered the room and asked me what I wanted. I told him about the sad plight of the wounded freedom fighters and asked him to come and to give them medical assistance. He asked me if I knew the exact location where the freedom fighters were hiding. I said that I knew. He then told me to go with a nurse to them and bring them secretly to a house. When they arrived at the house, he promised that he would come there to give them medical assistance. I agreed to his plan. He assigned a nurse who was affiliated with the liberation forces to come with me. She took some of the medical equipment that she might need and we set off.

We knew that the Israeli army had blockaded the populated area around the orchards to which we were going and that they were checking whomever entered the area. To better conceal ourselves and our reasons for entering the area, we wore traditional women's clothing and veils, so that only our eyes could be seen. Organizing the help from Dr. Rashad for the freedom fighters had taken more than two hours. Thus, I was not surprised to discover that the woman who was supposed to wait for us and bring us to the freedom fighters was not where I had told her to wait for us. I suspected that she had given up on us and gone home.

Inside the closed area, we first inquired where the wounded men were hiding. People did not want to tell us. Finally, we met Um Ahmed, the mother of a martyr with whom I was acquainted, and she told us that the wounded were concealed in the second orchard grove. We went there with her. While walking to the second orchard grove we discerned units of the Israeli army continuing their search of the entire area.

When we reached the second orchard grove, the nurse who had accompanied me refused to enter the orchard with us. She was very tense and scared. She told us that she would enter the grove only if we found someone there who was wounded and needed help. Um Ahmed and I entered the grove and quite soon encountered an injured man lying on the ground with a rifle at his side. He was wearing a military uniform, but he also had a rope around his neck. I bent down and sensed that his breath was very weak and that he could hardly move. I decided to take his rifle, and when I bent to pick it up he murmured the word "Palestine" and died. When she saw that the freedom fighter had died, Um Ahmed began to scream. I angrily told her to stop screaming immediately, lest the Israeli soldiers hear us and come. She stopped. I must admit that we were both very frightened.

The nurse had entered the orchard when she heard the screaming. I asked her to check if the freedom fighter was dead, and she confirmed that he was no longer alive. I told her to use her scissors to cut the rope around his neck, but she was so scared and trembled so much that she could not even use the scissors. Finally, I cut the rope with my teeth. We gathered his few belongings, including the rifle. I took a clean handkerchief from the nurse and covered his face. Later I learned that this freedom fighter had been wounded in the chest and had told his comrade to leave him where we found him, since he knew that he would soon die.

I decided to go look for the other freedom fighter, but the nurse announced that she had had enough and was going home. Angrily, I admonished her and notified her that she was going nowhere until we found the second freedom fighter. She responded that the area was large and included four orchards. She asked, "How can we find him in such a large area?" I notified her that I would search for him in all four orchards and that she would accompany me. She hesitated and finally complied. Um Ahmed stayed with us, and we three women began to seek the second freedom fighter.

We searched for a long time without success and were about to give up hope of finding anyone. Suddenly I heard a rasping breathing behind a fence of thorns. Someone was hidden there.

"Who are you?" I asked.

A man's voice answered, "I am Ibrahim Abu Wael."

My next question was: "Where are you from?"

"I am from the liberation forces, a member of the Husseini Brigade. My legs are wounded, bleeding a bit, and I cannot stand on them. The sheikh was here and bandaged them, but I still cannot stand well upon them."

I looked around and saw that the Israeli soldiers were not far off. The voice asked, "Is Ayoub dead?"

"Yes."

"Please find a way to get me out of the orchard as soon as possible," he said.

I called the nurse to enter the grove and come help me. She refused. A unit of the Israeli army was not far off, and she was afraid. Finally, I saw passing near us a man whose son had been killed by the Israelis. I called him and he agreed to help. We reached Ibrahim Abu Wael and decided to get him out of the area on a thorny path that was not known to the Israelis. The man went ahead and cut a path in the thorns and I helped Ibrahim limp along that path. The nurse followed us. Even though Ibrahim had been shot in both legs, God gave him strength to walk. At the end of the path Ibrahim and I hid in the undergrowth, and the man went off and brought back a donkey cart and a set of women's clothes. We did not need the nurse, so she returned to the hospital.

Ibrahim dressed in the women's clothes and lay on the cart. His face was covered with a veil and only his eyes showed. We hid the arms in his clothes. We walked the donkey and the cart to the checkpoint that the Israeli soldiers had set up. The man told the soldiers that his pregnant wife was on the cart, that she had birth pangs and was about to deliver, and that he and I were taking her to a doctor. The soldier let us through, and we walked the cart slowly to the town of Beit Lahia. The man brought a car and we brought Ibrahim to Jebalia Refugee Camp. We wanted to hide him in the school, but we noticed that units from the Israeli army were beginning to surround Jebalia Refugee Camp, so we smuggled Ibrahim out. Before he was smuggled out, a nurse bandaged him well and gave him medicine.

I should perhaps mention that at the time of this event I was not a member of any of the underground organizations that struggled for Palestinian freedom. But my participation in rescuing Ibrahim Abu Wael brought about my greater involvement in the struggle for Palestinian freedom. In the days that followed, I continued to help my aunt to distribute leaflets of the Palestinian Front for Liberation of Palestine (PFLP). Soon I received a message announcing that Ziad Husseini, a major leader of the PFLP, was proud of me. He insisted that I join his faction of the liberation forces, which I did. When I joined, I insisted on learning how to use firearms. During the months that followed, after Ibrahim Abu Wael recovered from his wounds, he and Ziad trained me on how to use weapons. The training was done secretly in well-concealed places. I learned to use a pistol, and Ziad gave me a small pistol as a present for my services to the cause. I learned to use and throw hand grenades, and to fire and use a machine gun. After a few months of such training, Ziad Husseini and Ibrahim

Abu Wael were very pleased with my ability to use firearms. They decided to let me participate in operations against the Israeli army. I soon did.

In 1971 we set up an ambush for a squad of Israeli soldiers who were on military patrol in Shatti Refugee Camp, which is adjoined to Gaza City. We threw grenades and homemade bombs at the soldiers and immediately retreated. I have no idea if any of the Israelis were hit. That was the first time I used firearms against the Israeli oppressors. The second time was when we ambushed some soldiers on the road to Jebalia Refugee Camp, near the graveyard. We hid in the graveyard and threw grenades at some soldiers who were passing by. After throwing the grenades, we immediately retreated. Again, I do not know if any of the Israeli soldiers were hit in our attack. We had a machine gun with us during this ambush, but we did not use it.

I was severely wounded in the third attack in which I participated, in 1972, again near Jebalia Refugee Camp. Our unit was told to attack during the holy month of Ramadan, and we fasted during the day. After we broke our fast at sunset, we set out at around 6:00 P.M. It was winter and already dark. We were four fighters in our military unit; the other three were men. Our goal was to throw hand grenades into a house and into an Israeli military intelligence car; we had information that in either the car or the house, an Israeli intelligence officer was holding a meeting with a Palestinian collaborator. Their meetings always took place near or in a house owned by a Palestinian officer who had left for Egypt in 1967. Supposedly the house was empty, but we suspected that they might be meeting there.

For this attack, I wore a khaki military uniform. I had hand grenades in my belt. My hair was covered by a round hat so that it would not interfere with my actions. My role was to throw the grenades into the house and into the Israeli intelligence car. The three men in our unit were supposed to cover me. We knew that near the Israeli military intelligence car there was usually a military car with soldiers guarding the intelligence officer who was meeting the collaborator. We did not know who the collaborator was. If we could recognize him during the mission, we were supposed to bring that information back to our organization and they would deal with him.

I neared the house quietly in the dark and threw a grenade into the window. It exploded and immediately the Israeli soldiers started shooting at me. I don't know where the shooting came from. When I moved toward the Israeli intelligence car in order to throw the second grenade, I was hit by bullets, first in the hand that held the grenade and then in the chest. The grenade was open and somehow I succeeded in throwing it in the direction of the Israeli vehicle. Before I fell, another bullet hit me in the abdomen. The second grenade exploded and there was much smoke and gunfire. Lying on the ground, I called out to the men in my unit that I was wounded and instructed them to leave me there and retreat. They retreated and after a few moments the shooting stopped.

In a short time, many units of the Israeli army arrived and surrounded the area. I lay there wounded, and a Palestinian woman stealthily approached me in the dark. She quietly asked me what she could do for me. I told her to go home, since nothing could be done. Before she left, she covered my wound with her handkerchief and told me, "You are pure."

Israeli soldiers found me lying on the ground, wounded and bleeding. At first, probably because of my uniform, they did not know whether I was a man or a woman. The Israeli military governor approached and asked me in Arabic who I was. I insulted him and told him that I was a woman. He and other soldiers lifted me onto a stretcher, put me on an Israeli vehicle, and took me to the UNRWA clinic in Jebalia Refugee Camp, which was the nearest medical clinic where I could get first aid. The Israeli military governor together with many soldiers came to the clinic to guard me and to see what was happening.

As I was lying in the clinic, in the women's section, a woman named Um Mohammed approached. She understood that I would be taken away by the Israelis after the doctors completed first aid treatment for my wounds. She told me that she could take my gold bracelets and hide them. I didn't want the gold to fall into the hands of the Israelis and told her to take my gold bracelets. I asked her to bring me some water, but when she went to bring a cup of water the Israeli officers caught her, hit her, and yelled at her not to come near me. Somehow Um Mohammed entered the room, and I told her that I was the daughter of Abu Samir El-Hilo. She was surprised since my father was well known. After being given first aid, the Israeli army brought an ambulance and decided to take me to Shiffa Hospital in Gaza City. I lost consciousness on the way.

I regained consciousness in Shiffa Hospital and told the doctor there not to heal me because I preferred to die rather than to fall into the hands of the Israeli oppressors. Since it was after 10:00 P.M., the operation room at Shiffa Hospital was closed. It seemed difficult to find a crew of Palestinian doctors and nurses to operate on me. The Israeli army officers feared for my life, and indeed I lost consciousness. They sent me in an ambulance to the Israeli army hospital in Tel Hashomer, inside Israel, not far from Tel Aviv. On the way to Tel Hashomer, which is about an hour and a half drive from Gaza City, an Israeli doctor and a medical crew accompanied me and treated me; they did everything to keep me alive. The Israeli doctor who accompanied me in the ambulance later told me that all the way I had murmured, "Land and honor."

At Tel Hashomer Hospital, I was operated on immediately by Israeli doctors and received the medical treatment that saved my life. When I regained consciousness, I found that I was linked to an infusion and other tubes, and my hair had been shorn. I was constantly guarded by Israeli soldiers. On one occasion, these soldiers who guarded me forcefully repulsed an attack on me by a wounded Israeli soldier and members of his family. Evidently, the Israeli soldier who wished to harm me had been wounded from one of the grenades that I had thrown.

While still in the intensive care unit of the hospital, I was told that my right hand must be amputated under the elbow. I knew that my hand had been hit by a bullet; I signed a document that allowed them to amputate my hand so as to save my life. I lost track of time, but I believe that I was hospitalized in Tel Hashomer Hospital for seventeen days. The doctors at the hospital were dedicated to my well-being. Officers of the Israeli security service, the Shabak, tried to interrogate me during the first days that I was in Tel Hashomer Hospital, while I was still lying half conscious in the intensive care unit. But the doctors discerned that they were disturbing me, and they did not allow them to interrogate me.

Soon after my being transferred from the intensive care unit to a regular ward in the hospital, two interrogators from the Shabak came to me while I was lying in bed. I was in pain, suffering from my wounds and hardly conscious of what was going on. The officers of the Shabak immediately threatened me that they would have all my teeth pulled out if I did not confess everything and tell them all about my activities in our military organization. They also threatened me that they would not allow the doctors to give me blood, and so I would die. I mumbled that it was all right with me, I was willing to die. They told me that they would not allow my family to meet with me. I was silent. They left and returned on the morrow. Every day they came, for a week or so. I kept silent.

Finally, during one of the meetings with the officers of the Shabak, when they discerned that I was feeling a little better, one interrogator put a tool into my mouth while I was lying on the hospital bed and demanded that I agree to speak. Otherwise, he notified me, he would pull out my teeth. I pushed him away and the tool cut a deep wound inside my mouth. I screamed and the nurses and doctors came running. When the doctors saw the blood streaming from my mouth and learned that the interrogators had wounded me deliberately, they were very angry. The Israeli doctors told the interrogators to leave, which they did. They did not return as long as I was in Tel Hashomer Hospital.

Later the doctors let me know that they had decided to send the interrogators away and not allow them to meet me as long as I was hospitalized. The doctors at the hospital also sent me to an Israeli specialist who treated the wound in my mouth, and it slowly got better. Because of the wound that the interrogators had inflicted, I could not speak for four days, and for weeks my mouth hurt. When representatives of the International Red Cross visited me in the hospital, I told them about what the officers of the Shabak had done to me. Moshe Dayan, the Israeli defense minister, also visited me in the hospital. He told me that he considered me a military prisoner, who could be exchanged. I understood that it meant that I had obtained a special status.

When I recovered a bit and could be discharged from the hospital, an Israeli ambulance with guards in it and an accompanying military patrol in a jeep brought me to Gaza Central Prison in Gaza City. I was still weak, and the officers of the Shabak in the prison told the guards immediately to isolate me from other women and to put me in a cell alone. The guards took me to an isolated cell with no bed. After they left, through the small barred windows of the cell I told people in other cells who I was and asked them whether members of my family were also imprisoned. They told me that the Israelis had also arrested my mother, father, aunt, and cousin. These members of my family were jailed in the cells on another floor of the prison. The Israelis first gave me a flea-infested straw mattress on the floor, but I refused to lie on it. Finally they brought me a leather mattress. I slept on it and used my shoes as a pillow. It was quite a change from the clean hospital room and the bed in Tel Hashomer.

That evening, I demanded to see the commander of the prison. The next morning I was led into his office. I told him that I was wounded and perhaps even a military prisoner, as Moshe Dayan had said. That status entitled me to rights, and unless he provided me with what I should receive as a human being, I would file a complaint against him. I demanded that I receive a pillow and a spoon, so that I would not have to eat with my hands. I also wanted a curtain, so that all the male guards in the corridor could not see me when I was in a modest situation. The commander of the prison responded that since I was a special case, he could provide me with a pillow, a spoon, and a curtain. I then said that all prisoners deserved such minimal respect for their rights and that they should receive what I receive. He refused.

In response, I told the prison commander that I did not want to be singled out for better treatment and that he could keep his pillow, spoon, and curtain. The prison commander told the guards to return me to my cell. Some days later representatives of the International Red Cross visited us in the prison to check up on our conditions. I told them about our demands. After their visit, suddenly, all prisoners were provided with pillows and spoons, and female prisoners were allowed to hang curtains in their cells, behind which they could attend to their intimate bodily needs.

Despite my still being weak and sick, my interrogation began almost immediately. In those days, 1972, when the officers of the Shabak supposedly interrogated a person, they always started by beating and torturing the prisoner. Few questions were asked; there was no cleverness or subtlety to the interrogation. Just beating, beating, and beating; pain, pain, and more pain; torture, torture, and more torture.

On the third day of my interrogation, the so-called interrogators beat me on the head with their fists while spraying me with boiling water and ice water. Suddenly I felt terrible pains in my head and collapsed. The interrogators had me carried to the prison doctor, who discovered that my eye was bleeding internally. He did not know what to do and sent me to an Israeli military hospital; the Israeli doctor there said that I needed immediate surgery. Thus, I was returned in an ambulance to the Israeli hospital at Tel Hashomer. But the expert physicians at Tel Hashomer could not save my eye. I am since then blind in one eye, as a result of Israeli torture. After two days of treatment at Tel Hashomer Hospital, I was returned to the Gaza Central Prison in Gaza City. My interrogation and torture were resumed.

Torture now included fewer beatings. Instead, the Israeli officers did not let me sleep, or forced me to stand on one leg for hours, or put me in a tight closet where I could not sit or move and had me stand there for hours, or let me lie down and sleep but tied my hands to my body and my hair to the window bars, so that whenever I fell asleep my hair was pulled and hurt. They also refused to let me go to the bathroom to relieve myself. Once when I was weak from torture, the Israelis put me into a refrigerator, which was very cold. I fainted and do not even know how long I was in the refrigerator, because when I regained consciousness I was in a regular cell. They also gave me disgusting food, which was impossible to eat. I lost many kilograms of my weight and looked like a walking skeleton. By forcing us to lose our bodily strength, they probably believed that our determination would be lessened. With me it didn't happen.

The officers of the Shabak also threatened me that they would remove all my clothes and bring a big black man to rape me if I did not confess. And indeed, the male interrogators from the Shabak forced me to undress in front of them. After I undressed, they took my clothes and announced that only after I confessed would my clothes be returned. I was defiant. I was not afraid of being raped, since my aunt had told me, before I was involved in military activities, that this threat was never implemented. Still, being forced to stand naked in front of my interrogators wounded my honor and self respect.

Our society is conservative, and forcing women to undress in front of male interrogators is an especially evil form of torture. I know that there were Palestinian women who confessed about their involvement in our struggle for freedom after being forced to remove their clothes during interrogation. One of them told me that she felt so abused by being forced to stand naked in front of her interrogators, she was willing to confess anything.

During my verbal interrogation, they confronted me with the confessions of some of my comrades, which implicated me. I believe that these comrades confessed because they were told that I had been killed. Thus, the interrogators tried to convince me to confess about various activities in which I had participated. I refused to talk about anything except the military operation in which I was wounded. After much torture, I confessed that I had participated in that operation. The interrogation took three months, and I was not allowed to see anyone except my lawyer and representatives of the International Red Cross. Probably because of my poor health, the interrogation and torture were halted for a period of six months. During that six-month period of incarceration, my health improved and I was allowed to receive a few visits from my family.

After that respite, I was again interrogated for a few weeks. Finally, I was charged formally in an Israeli military court. The charges were: participation in a military operation in which Israeli soldiers were killed, illegal possession of weapons, and membership in a terrorist organization. The military court convened in Gaza City and I was represented by one of the leading lawyers in the Gaza Strip, Fayez Abu Rachma. My prosecutors were Israeli military officers who were lawyers, and the judges were three Israeli military officers. Since I had confessed, the trial was quite short, about ten sessions. The lawyers were dealing mainly with formalities.

Because Israeli soldiers had been killed in the military operation, the prosecutors demanded the death penalty, even though Israeli law did not permit the death penalty. My lawyer pointed out that I had lost my hand and had been tortured and blinded in one eye by the interrogators; my health had been ruined as a result of torture during my interrogation. In short, he stated forcefully that my human rights had been abused and violated by the Israeli military regime. He also told the court that my family had been harassed by the Israeli authorities and had suffered for no reason. For instance, the Israelis had for no clear reason demolished my parents' house in Jebalia Refugee Camp. The court sentenced me to serve a seventeen-year prison sentence and also pay a fine of 2,000 shekels. Needless to say, I did not pay the fine. Probably because I had lost an eye, ten years of the seventeen-year prison sentence were suspended; hence my sentence was for seven years.

The first two years I was imprisoned in the Gaza Central Prison in Gaza City. After those years, I was moved to Ramleh Prison inside Israel. I spent much of the time in prison studying. One area of study was about revolutions against imperialist countries; for instance I read books that described the history of the resistence to imperialism in Algeria and Vietnam. I was not a leader in prison. There were older, qualified Palestinian women who led us and also taught us. I also studied psychology under their guidance.

After about four years in prison, I decided to affiliate myself with the Democratic Front for the Liberation of Palestine (DFLP), under the leadership of Nayef Hawatmah. My political links with the PFLP had never been strong. I was mainly linked to their military organization through the links that I described with Ziad Husseini, their commander in the Gaza Strip. But Ziad Husseini had died while I was in prison, and his military organization was no longer strong. In addition, I felt that the platform and the program for action of the DFLP were closer to my own views.

My health continued to deteriorate. In 1976, I was so sick that the prison medical staff told the authorities to release me. The Israeli doctors in Ramleh Prison believed that I would soon die; they gave me a month to live. When they heard this death verdict, the prison authorities decided to release me. I suspect that they preferred that I die at home or in a Palestinian hospital, and not in an Israeli jail.

On the day of my release, quite a few people came to receive me at the gates of Ramleh Prison. I saw that they were shocked when they perceived the state of my health. Indeed, I was very weak. After speaking briefly to these people and to members of my family, I was transferred for further treatment to Mukassed Hospital in Jerusaelm, which is the best Palestinian hospital.

At Mukassed Hospital I received excellent treatment, which probably saved my life. I still had a bullet in my leg, which caused much pain. They removed the bullet. They also treated the area of my lost eye, which was causing pain and frequent headaches. After that, I received additional medical treatment in Jordan. Slowly I recuperated and my strength returned. I began to be politically active for Palestinian freedom while I was recuperating in Jordan. In late 1977, the DFLP decided to secretly send me to Baghdad for military training. There, for some months I underwent military training, which included learning how to make bombs. But my health was not good, and I returned to Jordan for additional treatments and a period of recuperation.

In 1979, despite my poor health, I returned to the Gaza Strip and started organizational work for the DFLP. The work consisted of setting up cells of our organization and providing military training for the men in these cells. My health was often not very good, so I did not succeed much in my endeavors. I did travel every so often to Jordan to discuss plans and exchange information with our people there. I had a false Israeli identification card and used two names so as to avoid suspicion during these trips. Once I spent four months in Jordan using the false name. Despite these measures to conceal our activities, they were uncovered by the Israeli military authorities, and at the beginning of 1981 many members of the DFLP were arrested by the Israeli military. It turned out that the Israeli interrogators knew about my trips to Jordan, including those trips that I took with a false identification card.

The Israeli interrogators began their interrogation by asking me about my military activities and my trips to Jordan. I responded that I had gone to Jordan for medical treatment. They concluded that I would tell them nothing and decided to torture me. I was put in solitary confinement for two and a half months in Gaza Central Prison. My torture consisted of frequent harsh beatings. In addition, they would make me stand for long periods facing a naked Palestinian man who was accompanied by a dressed man. While this was occurring they would try to strip me, but I didn't let them. They retreated when I violently refused to be stripped. The naked man told me once that I should understand his situation of being forced to stand naked in front of me. Another manner of torture was to handcuff me and tie me to a door for hours. Once I succeeded in untying myself, but the response was a harsh beating and being tied more securely. After three months of torture, I was released. I had not been charged with any crime.

After my release, despite my poor health and my being weak from the months of torture, I continued with my political and military activities. I endeavored to organize cells of freedom fighters and train them to oppose the Israeli occupation. But during that short period, my bad health did not allow more than laying the foundation for opposition to the occupation. The Israelis arrested me again in the late summer of 1981, and this time, after being tortured, I was put on trial for organizing military opposition to the Israeli forces. Someone who received arms from us or provided arms for us must have broken down during interrogation and mentioned my name. The torture I underwent went on for about three months; it was similar to what I have already described. In addition to the beatings, I remember the interrogators forcing me to strip;

they then called the guards and instructed them to pour ice-cold water on me and to make me to sit for hours half-naked and wet in a very cold room, which was called the refrigerator.

In my trial, I was found guilty of participating in military activities against the Israeli regime. I was sentenced to five years in prison, of which two and a half years were suspended. I was released from prison in 1984. With my release, I renewed my activities against the Israeli military occupation. My focus, however, was now on political activities. I participated in a few training courses in the West Bank that were organized for members of our leadership.

After completing the courses, a leading member of our party, Yousef Al-hamalawi, and I were appointed to be responsible for all DFLP's political and educational activities in the Gaza Strip. Together with other women, I helped to establish a women's organization that would provide educational services for the population in the Gaza Strip. This organization grew and in the late 1980s we numbered 700 women. Our endeavors had some success, and before the intifada we had opened twenty-one kindergarten classes and ten classes for illiterate adults in which they learned to read and write. We also established seventeen centers of the DFLP, which were spread all over the Gaza Strip; at the centers, local people met to discuss political issues and to initiate activities such as opening a kindergarten. We also organized about ten women's groups where women met in order to arouse their awareness of the political situation in which we were oppressed. These activities continued until the summer of 1990, when again I was arrested together with Yousef Alhamalawi.

The story of my arrest this time is intriguing. We had urged Yousef Alhamalawi to get married to a member of our party, the DFLP. After they married, their home became our headquarters for the entire Gaza Strip. Our files were there, and we would often meet there to discuss our political activities. One day in the early summer of 1990, a member of our party was driving me in his car to Yousef's home. We had important files with us. We suddenly noticed that we were being watched and followed. I told the man to drive to my grandfather's house, which was close by. He quickly did. I unloaded the files in my grandfather's house and the driver and I fled.

An Israeli squad of soldiers soon entered my grandfather's house. They were looking for me. They searched the house and found and took the files I had left. After this incident, the Israeli army started searching for me intensively. I evaded being arrested by many means, including sleeping in different homes in different parts of the Gaza Strip. They finally did catch me, and what happened on that day is the intriguing story that I want to tell.

I had moved to Dir Elbalah, a village in the center of the Gaza Strip, which was less dangerous than Gaza City. For three days before the day of my arrest, I had noticed a red car with a Gaza license plate turning up wherever I was. On the day I was arrested, I was being driven back from Gaza City to Dir Elbalah in the afternoon, in a car with my sister and her young children. The car was stopped at an Israeli army checkpoint and a soldier came up to the car. He was holding a photograph of me and looked into the car. He looked carefully at me and at the photograph and said, "Please get out of the car, Nema."

My sister and I got out of the car. I told the soldier, "My name is not Nema. I am Myasar, Nema's sister. Nema looks like me." The soldier asked me for my identification card. I told him, "My identification card is not with me; I forgot it at home."

The soldier phoned his commander, who told him not to release me. His commander instructed him to tell me to sit in the Israeli army tent near the army checkpoint, guarded by other Israeli soldiers, while the car that brought me was to drive to my home and bring back the identification card that would prove that I was Myasar and not Nema. I sat down at the opening of the tent on a bench, guarded by two Israeli soldiers. My sister and the car drove off to get the identification card. A lawyer who I knew, called Abu Shaban, passed the checkpoint at that moment. I succeeded in stopping him and indicating to him what was happening. I asked him to remain with me, which he did.

A few moments after I remained alone with Abu Shaban, guarded by the soldiers, the suspicious red car that had been following me for three days arrived at the checkpoint. A Palestinian man sitting in the car opened the window and said, "Nema." I did not answer.

The Palestinian man came out of the red car, entered the tent, and turned to me again. I refused to talk to him, and covered my ears with my hands. He then went to his car and removed the Gaza license plate. Underneath it was an Israeli yellow license plate, with a Jerusalem label. In the next few moments something weird happened. The driver of the red car approached and told me that if I got into his car he would help me escape. The Israeli soldiers who were supposedly guarding me were willing to let me enter the Palestinian's red car and escape; they even forcefully distanced the lawyer, Abu Shaban, from me.

I notified the Palestinian that I would not get into the red car with him. I understood that he was a collaborator and once I got into the car he would shoot me and notify the Israeli authorities that I was killed while trying to escape. I suddenly recognized him as Abu Duhair from a well-known family in Rafah. I screamed to Abu Shaban to come help me and told him that Abu Duhair was trying to arrange a situation whereby he could shoot me for trying to escape. Luckily, while this was going on, three additional lawyers from Gaza City arrived at the checkpoint. Abu Shaban called to them and asked them to join him in guarding me. They came to stay with me, and the soldiers stopped encouraging me to enter the red car. The new lawyers started inquiring what was happening. After a few moments the commander of the Israeli Army Civil Administration arrived. He knew me very well from many previous incidents and meetings.

The commander of the Civil Administration got out of his car, came up to me, and said, "You are welcome, Miss Nema. What is the problem?" I responded, "If you want to arrest me, you can take me to the prison legally. You don't have to play dirty tricks."

He looked at me and asked, "Which dirty tricks?" I pointed to Abu Duhair, who was standing near his red car. The commander looked in that direction and said, "Don't worry about that dog."

The commander of the Civil Administration arranged for Israeli soldiers to take me legally to prison, with a woman soldier guarding me. The lawyers who were at the checkpoint guarding me also came to the prison to make sure that I arrived safely.

After forty-five days of being imprisoned, I learned that Abu Duhair had been murdered and his body cut up into pieces. The pieces of his cut-up body had been delivered to his family in a sack. While I was being interrogated, the interrogators gave me the information of his death and asked me what I knew about it. I knew nothing. The Israelis spread the story that our freedom fighters had killed him. I believe that he was killed by the Israelis, since after the incident with me at the Israeli army checkpoint he was useless to them; indeed, after that incident, everyone knew that he was a collaborator. I believe that the Israelis organized Abu Duhair's death so that it would look like an act of Palestinian revenge.

I was put on trial, again in a military court, and was charged with organizing illegal political activities against the Israeli regime. I was sentenced to eighty-five months in jail, but forty months were suspended. I was released in 1994, after forty-five months in jail. My release occurred during the peace process. Many people from all Palestinian parties came to congratulate me upon my release from prison.

Now I want to dedicate my life to humanitarian work for our Palestinian people and helping Palestinian women and refugees attain their legal and human rights. I am employed and active in a few organizations which are dedicated to these goals. We receive financial support from international foundations. I do not want to be part of the formal Palestinian Authority. I hope that the peace process will help the Palestinian people obtain their legitimate rights. Like other members of my political party, I believe that Yasser Arafat is working for our legitimate rights and I support him.

Chapter 7

Taher Shriteh

I was born in 1960 in Gaza City to parents who were refugees. My grandfather and his family had fled to the Gaza Strip during the 1948 War from the town of Yebna in the newly established state of Israel. Now the Israeli town of Yavneh occupies that area. Fortunately, my grandfather had some money, with which he purchased a small, rather ugly house in the Shajaya neighborhood in Gaza City, in which the family resided until 1951.

My father was the only one of my grandfather's sons who survived childhood. My grandfather had two brothers, who, as young men, joined the Turkish army in the period when the Ottomans ruled the Middle East; over the years all contact with them was lost. Thus, my extended family was not large. My father married when he was seventeen or eighteen years old. My mother came from a branch of the extended Shriteh family which is close to the branch of my father. Many members of her branch of the family reside in East Jerusalem. Because my father's family was not large, my parents wanted many children, and indeed we are seven brothers and five sisters. Our small extended family may be one of the reasons that I feel close to my siblings.

During the period of the British Mandate in Palestine, which ended in 1948, my father learned to be a male nurse and medic who could serve village people. He was very helpful in curing eye infections. He also dressed simple wounds or gave medical relief for aches and pains. Difficult cases were referred to the hospital. After completing his studies, he was appointed by the British government to serve in the Arab villages in the Yebna area. He received some payment from the sick to whom he attended. Cash was rare. Usually, the people whom he attended gave him farm products such as eggs, bread, or a chicken.

When my grandparents, parents, and their children fled to the Gaza Strip and later moved into the small house that had been purchased by my grandfather, they found it very difficult to make a living and to live in the small house. My father found a job working as a nurse for UNRWA. He earned between $200 and $300 a month, which is a meager sum for a large family. We did not discuss these problems since my father was a reticent person. He seldom spoke more than a few words. He smoked incessantly, which proved very unfortunate. He died of lung cancer in October 1987 when he was fifty-nine years old.

The family house in which we all lived during my childhood was indeed small. There was one large bedroom for all of us, that is, for twelve children, and a small bedroom for my parents. The house was built by my grandfather in 1951 in the sand dunes that then surrounded Gaza City. As children of refugees, we attended an UNRWA school. We lived in poverty. I had no shoes, and I shared my only pair of sandals with my brother, Zaher. Due to a lack of school buildings in the Gaza Strip, there were two sessions of school in each building: a morning session and an afternoon session. I would walk the kilometer and a half to school in the morning wearing sandals; I would return home as soon as school let out so as to give the sandals to Zaher. He put on the sandals and hurried to school in order to study in the afternoon session.

Never was I given new clothes. Everything that I wore was secondhand, and often it was patched. My mother would manage to sew clothes for all of us from discarded clothes that were given to her. Our poverty was not exceptional among refugees. However, I did have a friend whose father was a driver and whose level of material existence was much better than ours. I was not very successful in my first year at school, and the teacher often beat me with a rod made of bamboo. Only in the second grade did I begin to excel in my studies; by the end of the second grade, I was among the best pupils in the class.

My mother was illiterate and had never learned the rudiments of reading and writing. She was totally unable to relate to my school studies or my intellectual development. In addition, my father rarely spoke. He would leave for work before 7:00 in the morning and return after 2:00 in the afternoon. At home, he would sit without speaking and smoke and drink tea or coffee. He would often receive patients in our home and give them medical care or advice.

The mattresses upon which we slept were made of small pieces of discarded clothes. We always suffered from cold. Since we were refugees, every month we received some food from UNRWA. On an announced morning each month, my brothers and I would go to the food distribution center of UNRWA, where representatives of all refugee families in our neighborhood gathered. We would be arranged in groups according to the place in Palestine, now Israel, where we had resided before becoming refugees. The food that UNRWA distributed was flour, oil, sugar, and tin cans of meat. For vegetables and fruits, we children would go to the market and buy the least-expensive fruits or vegetables that were on sale; quite often they were half rotten. We never purchased our underwear. My mother would carefully cut the sacks in which UNRWA distributed flour into pieces that fit our body; she would then sew the pieces together and make our underwear.

My brothers and I knew that we were poor and that we had to help support the family by working during the school vacations. The money we earned would help us to buy used clothes for the school year. When I was seven years old, during school vacations I worked in a small factory which made chairs and received as payment the amount of half a dollar a week. Later, during school vacations I sold newspapers, sunflower seeds, and ice cream in the street. I earned very little. One year I earned some money by helping people clean out trash. All these jobs brought in very little money, but we all sensed that even earning small amounts would somehow assist us to alleviate our poverty.

When I reached the age of thirteen, I felt that I was a man and must go find work in Israel where wages were much higher. This decision was an important moment in my life. During summer vacation, I would arise at 2:00 A.M. and walk six kilometers with my fourteen-year-old brother and a sixteen-year-old neighbor to the Nachal Oz checkpoint where we could cross over into Israel. Near the checkpoint was what we called a "slave camp." It was an area where Palestinian workers waited for Israeli employers and their pickup trucks to come and take them to do a day's work in Israel, mainly weeding and harvesting crops. The pickups would come and we young boys would try to get on the back of the small truck so as to be taken to work in the Israeli farms in the Negev. Usually I failed to get a job. The Israeli driver wanted older, stronger, more experienced workers. But, every so often I would be taken to work, which was usually hard and backbreaking.

In those jobs, I weeded and gathered onions, weeded sunflowers, gathered watermelons, and weeded and gathered tomatoes. Gathering watermelons was especially difficult, because it meant picking them and throwing them onto a slowly moving truck. Many watermelons weighed fifteen pounds or more. I was usually hungry and thirsty during the toil, but we were allowed to drink water only when we finished a row; in addition, the food that I had brought from home did not appease my hunger. I would earn between ten and twelve dollars a day. At times, however, we would be cheated and not paid. There were also small prizes. Often, when we gathered watermelons, our employer allowed us to take one or two watermelons home; carrying one or two watermelons made the six-kilometer walk in the evening from the Nahal Oz checkpoint to my home even more exhausting. After eating supper, I would immediately fall asleep so as to get up at 2:00 A.M. on the morrow and go to seek work again.

When I reached the age of sixteen, I decided to seek work in construction in Tel Aviv. I was not very successful and rarely found a job. One day, however, an Israeli man said he was looking for two men to load a truck with sacks of lime. I immediately volunteered, and he took me. I was wearing a thin shirt, and as I loaded the truck, sweat poured out, wetting my shirt completely. I received twenty-five dollars for my work, but on the way home I felt that my back was burning. The lime had caused me terrible burns. I was sick for three weeks because of my burned back, shoulders, and arms, and I still have scars.

The following summer I found work for a few months in the kitchen of a bar and restaurant in Tel Aviv. Every day, starting in the afternoon, I washed dishes and did other chores until 4:00 the following morning; then the restaurant and bar would close and I would sleep on a mattress in the kitchen. I was not allowed to leave the kitchen when customers were in the bar because they did not like to see an Arab man in a place where they went to enjoy themselves. The owner paid me what he had promised as a salary for the first two months. At the end of the third month, however, I was kicked out without pay. I went to complain to the Israeli police station that was nearby, but the police officer in charge told me to get out of his sight.

The next summer I worked for an elderly Jewish couple whose business was buying and selling chairs and tables. I did all the lifting, loading, and unloading of their goods. They liked me and were nice to me. They paid me at the end of every day of work.

I completed high school in 1978 with very good grades. The Egyptian government awarded 500 scholarships each year for university studies in Egypt to the best students in the Gaza Strip. The scholarships allowed the students to study without paying tuition. I wanted to be a medical doctor. I applied to thirty-two medical schools all over Egypt and also to the Department of Agriculture in Cairo University. I was accepted to study agriculture. I studied four years at Cairo University. My family supported me financially; they paid for my living expenses. My grades were excellent. During the summer vacations, I continued to work, either in the Gaza Strip or as a laborer in Israel.

In 1983 I graduated with a bachelor's degree in agricultural engineering, but I could not find work as an agricultural engineer. The Egyptian regime refused to employ Palestinians, since Egypt had a large surplus of indigenous laborers. The Israeli army officers, who were in charge of the civil administration in the Gaza Strip, were clear as to the conditions for getting a job. They told me that if I would work as a collaborator for the Israeli military they would give me a job in the public administration of the Gaza Strip. Of course, I refused to be a collaborator.

The only job that I could find was to be the cashier of a small ice cream firm in Gaza City, which belonged to a distant cousin. My salary was $100 a month. After three months, I was fed up with the work and was not pleased with the salary. I applied for a tourist visa at the United States consulate in Tel Aviv and was surprised when I received a visa to enter the United States. My brother borrowed money from our neighbors for my one-way ticket to the United States.

I lived in the United States for two and a half years. At first, I enrolled in a program for a master's degree in mechanical engineering at the University of Wisconsin in Milwaukee. But my funds were insufficient, and I could not continue my studies. I had to start working at cleaning jobs in a supermarket, which was difficult. Finally, I quit graduate school.

During the period that I worked at low-paying jobs in the United States, I shared an apartment with a Jewish young man. Our relations were good. We did not discuss politics. Once, however, when a Jewish friend of his was present, they started talking about the Middle East and they derided the Arabs. I was appalled at their ignorance concerning what was happening in the Middle East. I explained to them how the Palestinians were oppressed and exploited by the Israelis, and presented some very painful details about our continual suffering. They were both very surprised at what I disclosed. The incident showed me that there was much ignorance in the United States about what was happening in the Gaza Strip and in Palestine. Members of the Jewish community shared that ignorance.

That difficult encounter was a turning point in my life. I recognized that the harsh crimes that Israel commits against the Palestinian people in the Occupied Territories are very much concealed from the American public. The media in the United States intentionally do not publish the truth about the Israeli-Palestinian conflict. Furthermore, the people in the United States hardly know the amount of aid that the United States government continually sends to Israel while it continues to daily oppress and exploit the Palestinian people.

I became aware that I would not succeed in developing a career in the United States. I missed my parents, siblings, and friends in the Gaza Strip. In 1986, after more than two years in the United States, I returned to the Gaza Strip. I started working at odd jobs which did not bring in much money. I would purchase clothes in Jerusalem and sell them to retail stores in the Gaza Strip. I worked a bit as a taxi driver but did not make much since I sympathized with many poor people and did not charge them for the ride. I wrote a few articles on agriculture in Arabic for a local newspaper.

In early 1987, I decided to visit Egypt, which, since my studies, I regarded as a second home. I spent some days there, and on the day that I returned to Gaza City, my mother called me on the phone from East Jerusalem, where her family resided. She notified me that she had found a wonderful bride for me. She asked me to come to Jerusalem in order to meet the woman. I was almost twenty-seven years old. According to the norms of our society, I should have been married for a few years already. People were saying that since I was unmarried, perhaps there was something not good about me. In our society, marriage is still very much arranged by the families involved. For instance, it is impossible to date a woman without involving her family.

I traveled to East Jerusalem and met Zahra. Her name means "flower." I must say that she was the first woman whom I wished to marry. She is from a wise, good family. For years I had wanted to marry a woman who could think independently and not only rely on me. By thinking independently, I felt, such a woman could help me in my life and our life together would be worthy. Zahra is such a woman. In her family there are eight sisters.

When I arrived in Jerusalem at Zahra's home, everything went according to our accepted customs. I sat with her parents and brothers in the living room and chatted. After a while, Zahra entered with a tray on which were tea and coffee; she went from one to another and we helped ourselves. She then sat down and joined us. When the woman who is eligible to be married joins the group, there is an awkward moment. It is well known that only the courageous suitor decides to speak to the woman who may be his wife. I acted courageously. Among other topics, we spoke of the period during which I lived in the United States.

Our first meetings, before we became engaged, were always with intermediaries from our families present, either with us or in the next room with the door between the rooms open. After several such meetings, during which we spoke at length and learned a bit about each other, Zahra and I decided to become engaged. After that decision, we could take walks together and be more alone. We continued to meet and after about eight months we married—on August 20, 1987.

During the period before I married, I had no regular work. My habit of reading many newspapers and political leaflets helped me to become a journalist. I read an advertisement that an Arabic newspaper that was published in Nazareth needed a reporter in the Gaza Strip. I responded to the advertisement and said that I had written a few articles for the Arab press. I was invited to Nazareth for a meeting with the editor. I became their reporter for 350 shekels ($150) a month. For that sum, I also had to distribute their newspaper in Gaza City. Because I had no car, I would distribute it by foot. Through my work, I became acquainted with other reporters and also started making contacts.

In October 1987, I was sitting in the office of a reporter friend, Daoud Kuttab, in East Jerusalem, waiting for him. He had left on an errand. Suddenly, a person entered who was looking for someone who spoke English. We spoke for half an hour and he turned out to be Bernard Edinger, deputy chief of Reuters News Agency in Israel. I told Bernard that his agency does not present the situation in the Gaza Strip correctly and that the Gaza Strip has been ignored by international news agencies. He explained that Reuters did not know of a person who resided in the Gaza Strip and could be their reporter. It did not occur to me, during our discussion, that I would become the Reuters representative in the Gaza Strip and a professional journalist.

When Daoud Kuttab returned, Bernard suggested that we go to a restaurant. I was a bit naive and mixed up, since I did not have enough money with me to pay for a meal in a good restaurant. When I hinted about my financial situation they laughed good-heartedly, and Bernard invited me. As a result of that meeting, I began accompanying foreign journalists who wanted to report from the Gaza Strip. At first I accompanied Paul Taylor, chief of Reuters News Agency. Later I received a salary of $100 a month from Reuters News Agency and was paid around $50 for each day that I helped a foreign journalist. In November 1987, Paul Taylor asked me to work fully for him, reporting whenever there was news to be conveyed; he said that he could not pay me more than $400 a month including expenses, but he could send me other foreign journalists who would need someone to accompany them in the Gaza Strip and they would pay me for that day or days. He was true to his word, and a few days before the intifada, in early December 1987, Bob Simon from CBS News called me and said that he would like me to help him do a story on "The Gaza Strip—The Place Nobody Wants." I agreed to help him.

I borrowed a car from a member of my family. Bob Simon arrived with his television crew, who were Israelis, on the day that the intifada started, December 9, 1987. He wanted to go to the center of action, which was Jebalia Refugee Camp. In that camp, thousands of Palestinians had begun to demonstrate against the Israeli occupation. The Israeli soldiers were shooting at the Palestinian demonstrators. We reached the camp, and both the Israeli soldiers and the Palestinians were surprised to see a foreign television crew. I believe that the soldiers acted with restraint after they saw that we were filming their activities and their attempts to suppress the demonstration. That day I had helped to provide a scoop for CBS and for Reuters.

As the intifada spread throughout the Gaza Strip, I worked daily with Paul Taylor and Bob Simon, and they received immediate, accurate coverage of the events. When journalists from other stations and channels perceived that I could always lead Paul Taylor and Bob Simon to a crucial area of action, they started following our cars. During the early period of the intifada, they had no representatives in the Gaza Strip. At times, our two cars of CBS and Reuters would be followed by a dozen cars of other journalists, including the cars of Israeli reporters and journalists.

In those first weeks of the intifada, the Gaza Strip was like an erupting volcano, and many foreign journalists wanted to hire my services in order to get to the important stories. They knew that I had very little experience in journalism. During that initial period, I helped all the foreign reporters. I would translate for them when they interviewed people and arrange meetings with lay people and with leaders of various factions. At times, I would drive them to their meetings and the places they wished to visit, convey to them the background of the topic they were investigating, and brief them about the persons they were meeting for an interview. I would often suggest questions or propose places that were worth visiting.

As I learned more about journalism, my fields of activity broadened. I began reporting for BBC Radio, both in the Arabic and the English broadcasts. I helped CBS News produce programs and often helped them with the filming of programs. I wrote up news reports for Reuters News Agency. Most of the time my reports were in English, but at times they were in Arabic. I also photographed for Reuters. In addition, I would write reports for *Al-Quds*, an Arabic daily newspaper that comes out in Jerusalem.

After a while, I decided to seek a permanent position with a news agency. Although I also had worked for ABC News in the first few weeks of the intifada, I had to choose between them and CBS News. I decided to work for CBS News with Bob Simon.

When the intifada broke out, many shops and store owners in Gaza City decided to strike and close their shops for at least half a day. That was their way of participating in the rebellion against the Israeli occupation. The Israeli army was very much against this merchants' strike. They tried to convince the striking shopkeepers to keep the shops open all day long. They failed. In order to punish the shopkeepers who were striking, the army commander sent soldiers to weld shut the doors of the shops that had participated in the strike. Once the doors were welded closed, the shop owners could not enter their shops on the morrow. One day in January 1988, during the intifada, I was with Bob Simon and his crew as they were filming a team of Israeli soldiers who were welding shut the doors of some Palestinian shops. I stood nearby.

Suddenly the Israeli commander of the Gaza Strip, Lieutenant Colonel Yoseph Zeev, who was of Jewish-Yemenite origin and spoke Arabic, arrived on the scene. He approached us, accompanied by a coterie of Israeli officers and soldiers. We Palestinians felt that he considered himself to be the king of the Gaza Strip. He asked me in Arabic what I was doing there. I said I was a journalist from Gaza City who was working with CBS News. Lieutenant Colonel Zeev stared at me as if I was a terrorist and angrily said, "A journalist from Gaza City." He immediately asked me for my identification card and on the spot decided to arrest me. I firmly refused to be arrested, stating that I had done nothing wrong. At that moment, Bob Simon intervened and started yelling at Lieutenant Colonel Zeev, telling him to stop interfering with his work and that he needed me. Lieutenant Colonel Zeev got very angry and decided to arrest me by force. Bob Simon told me to go with them and promised me that he would not leave Gaza City until I was free.

Israeli soldiers took me to a small room in the Israeli government building and started to beat me. They knocked me around a bit and refused to allow me to go to the bathroom. In the meantime, Bob Simon sat outside and, true to his word, called the office of Yitzchak Rabin, the defense minister; Bob demanded that I be released immediately and that no harm be done to me. After six hours, the Israeli soldiers released me to go to sleep at home. They told me to return on the morrow. Bob Simon waited until I had been released and returned on the morrow to Gaza City; he waited another eight hours and made sure that the army formally released me.

I continued to work with foreign press organizations. I believe that my work angered the Israeli authorities. On February 1, 1988, they arrested me again, together with my brother Fakher, who is three years younger than I. Israeli soldiers took me to a military prison camp called Ansar II in Gaza City. The soldiers blindfolded me, tied my hands behind my back, and started to beat me. Since I was blindfolded, I could not see who was beating me.

Fortunately, that day Paul Taylor, the chief correspondent of Reuters News Agency in Israel, was supposed to meet me at Erez checkpoint, which is the northern entrance to the Gaza Strip from Israel. Paul was waiting for me to pick him up at Erez checkpoint. When I did not arrive, he called my home and learned from my brother Zaher, in broken Arabic, English, and Hebrew, that the Israeli army had arrested me. Like Bob Simon, he immediately complained to the Israeli authorities in the defense ministry. In the meantime, the Israeli soldiers had made Fakher and me remove our clothes, handcuffed us, and tied us outside in the wind and rain, so that we would suffer from the cold. They continued to beat and to kick us. After five hours of such torture, Fakher and I were released.

Before our release, the soldiers took Fakher and me to the office of the Israeli military commander of the prison. He said to me: "So you're a journalist. Well now you have a good story to report. Many journalists wanted to see it and write about it. Now you got the story and have had the experience." He was right. Paul wrote a good story about my arrest, and the story appeared in Reuters and was widely published. His story included many details which had not yet been exposed in the media about the newly established jail for protesters of the intifada, Ansar II.

The Israeli army decided to continually harass me. Every month or so they would arrest me for a few hours and interrogate me. After a few months of harassment, I was visiting a troubled area with Paul Taylor when we encountered Israeli soldiers with their commander, Lieutenant Colonel Zeev. They were shooting at Palestinian demonstrators. No journalists were allowed by the Israeli military to cover the demonstration. I was driving a newspaper delivery truck; Paul Taylor and his American photographer were in the car. I told the Israelis soldiers who had blocked off the area that I was delivering the local weekly newspaper. They looked into the truck and saw the stacks of newspapers and let us pass. Thus, Paul and his photographer got to report an exclusive story of the clashes.

The BBC decided to employ me on a regular basis in early 1988. The *New York Times* also decided to employ me as their representative in the Gaza Strip. The reason, I believe, for these successes was that I found ways of getting precise information and reporting it to these news agencies long before other journalists in the Gaza Strip.

Here is one story. One day in 1988, Paul Taylor called and told me that he had some information that Israel had moved tanks into the Gaza Strip. He wanted to know if the information was true; he asked for precise information as to how many tanks we could see, so that he could send in a report to Reuters News Agency. Paul said that as far as he knew, the army had unloaded the tanks in the area of Nuseirat Refugee Camp. I took my neighbor, Atiyah, to help me. I drove in my car to the area of the Israeli army camp in the area of Nuseirat Refugee Camp. Since we could perceive nothing from the main road, I turned into the road that led to the army camp and drove a kilometer up to the camp gate where Israeli soldiers stopped me with guns aimed at me. From the camp gate I could see the Israeli tanks, and as I stepped out of the car to speak to the soldiers, I told Atiyah to count the tanks and the military buses. I started talking in English to the soldiers, explaining that I believed I had come into the wrong road. They did not understand English and motioned to me, while speaking in Hebrew, to turn the car around and quickly leave the area. While talking to them, however, I had counted the Israeli tanks that could be seen in the camp. Atiyah had also counted and our results were equal. I drove back to the nearest phone and immediately reported the number of Israeli tanks that we had seen in that camp to Paul Taylor.

Here is another story. On November 15, 1989, when the PLO decided to declare a Palestinian State at its meeting in Algeria, the Israeli army declared a two-week-long curfew in the entire Gaza Strip. During the curfew, the Israeli army also cut off all telephone calls to and from the Gaza Strip. In a word, all the telephones in the Gaza Strip were dead; we were isolated from the world.

I wanted to report to the press agencies for whom I worked about this terrible and unjust curfew and about our reaction in the Gaza Strip to the declaration of a Palestinian State in Algeria. After four days of this unjust imprisonment of 800,000 people in their homes, I decided to try my luck at getting to a telephone. I thought that perhaps the telephones in the hospitals in Gaza City would be working. I took Zahra, who held our one-month-old baby boy in her arms. They sat beside me in the car and I started driving rapidly, crazily, in the direction of the nearest hospital for children, while blowing my horn. Once Israeli soldiers stopped me, aimed their guns at me, and asked why I was driving during the curfew—I told them, with great frustration, that my baby child was very sick and that I must get him to the hospital. The Israeli soldiers were very nervous and confused. I did not wait for them to contact their commander but drove straight to the hospital.

When I entered the hospital I met Abdallah Ayish, who was one of the leaders and heroes of the intifada. He was working in the hospital. I told him that I wanted to report what was happening in the Gaza Strip to the world press. He asked the nurse to let me use one of their telephone lines. For an hour, I reported to the foreign journalists with whom I worked about the terrible curfew, how the Palestinians survived during the curfew, and our response to what was happening in Algeria. We then carefully drove home.

Getting true, detailed, and precise information about the intifada was very complicated. In many parts of the Gaza Strip there were important activities against the occupation, yet they occurred in areas that had little contact with the outside world. Even today, many Palestinians in the Gaza Strip still live crowded in refugee camps in great poverty, without running potable water, without sewage, and without telephones. When the intifada broke out and in its early years, many of these impoverished people did not recognize the importance of using the international media in their daily struggle for freedom. In order to cope with this problem, and also in order that I, personally, not be seen at every newsworthy place—especially by Palestinian collaborators who reported to the Israeli security service—I enlisted helpers from all over the Gaza Strip. Some of my helpers worked as volunteers, and some received small payments.

Thus, after a few months, I had established a network of local helpers from all over the Gaza Strip, who reported directly to me as soon as they perceived that something newsworthy was happening. One consequence of my establishing this network of helpers was that my office became one of the major sources of information that served foreign journalists. We daily provided many foreign journalists with facts and figures about what was happening in the entire Gaza Strip. In passing on information, I always endeavored not to be politically involved in the events that occurred but rather to report the simple truth accurately.

My success as a journalist led to my being approached, in 1989 and 1990, by representatives of three Palestinian organizations that were active in the intifada. Each representative explained that his organization wanted to employ me, as a journalist, to support their political goals, or pay me to join their activities. I refused to negotiate with the representatives of all of the three parties. I explained to each of these representatives, whose work I respected, that I was faithful to the idea of an independent and free press—one that does not serve some political party. I stated that nothing that they might offer me would make me change my mind. Paul Taylor had explained to me that there was a fine line between good journalism and political involvement—a line of which I should be aware and should never cross. I believe that my refusal to receive money from these three organizations added to my honor.

On January 28, 1991, Israeli soldiers came to my house to arrest me. The reason had to do with my relationship with Yousef Hadad, who was in charge of relations with the media for the Islamic resistance movement, Hamas. Yousef was a lawyer. We had been close friends since our student days in Egypt, when we shared an apartment with a third friend in Cairo. Like people from other Palestinian organizations, Yousef would pass on to me all the information and news that he received. For instance, he would immediately send me important clandestine leaflets and statements that were supporting the Hamas. I received the material, reported what was newsworthy, and never asked Yousef any questions as to how he received the leaflets. That was a way of protecting myself. I understood that the less I knew about any of the Palestinian organizations that were participating in the struggle for our freedom, the healthier it was for me.

Yousef had an office where he worked as a lawyer, and in it was a facsimile machine. One day I asked Yousef to lend me his fax machine for a few days. Three days after he loaned me the fax, Yousef was arrested by the Israeli military forces. During his arrest, I returned the fax machine to his wife. The reason for my haste was that the Israeli army had decreed that it was illegal for a Palestinian to own or to operate a fax machine unless the army had given the Palestinian special permission. A week later the Israeli security service arrested me.

When I arrived at the prison, I was issued a pair of pants that did not fit me so my underwear showed, a shirt with only two buttons, and a pair of hard plastic sandals. Much of the time I was handcuffed, and my head was covered with a thick sack that reached my shoulders. The prison was packed with hundreds of Palestinian prisoners, and there were many Israeli guards. When I was arrested, Yousef's family sent the fax machine back to my house. That fax was like a hot potato—nobody wanted to be caught holding it. After a few days, two officers in the Israeli security service, the Shabak, took me, dressed in my ugly prison garb and blindfolded, to my house. A few armed Israeli soldiers accompanied us to make sure that I did not try to escape. Near the door they took the sack off of my head and removed my handcuffs. They knocked on the door and when Zahra answered, they asked my wife for the fax. Zahra said that there was no fax machine in my house. I then told Zahra quietly that there was no need to be brave and that she could give the Israelis the fax, which she did. I was then returned to prison so that the Shabak officers could continue to interrogate me.

They put me in a tiny cell in which the light was always on and there was no toilet. I was not allowed to go to the bathroom more than once a day, and then for less than a minute. I therefore decided not to eat or drink, so that I would not want to use a toilet. I drank and ate very little every day from what was served me. As a result, I lost fourteen kilograms of my weight during the thirty-eight days of my incarceration.

What interested the officers of the Shabak was how I received precise and immediate information about what was happening in the Gaza Strip. During my interrogation they repeatedly asked me how I got the information that I reported to the international press. I told them that unknown people called my office and gave me the information. The interrogators tortured me, demanding that I state that I was a member of Palestinian national organizations such as Fatah, Hamas, and the Communist Party—with no results. They also put a Palestinian collaborator in my cell, who tried to get incriminating information from me—but I had nothing to say and the trick failed. At times, I was so thirsty I could hardly speak during the interrogation, so they gave me some water. I was finally released from prison and formally charged with holding a facsimile machine and writing a book without permission. But the Israeli army decided to drop the charges when a well-known Israeli lawyer, Amnon Zichroni, who was hired by the *New York Times*, CBS News, and Reuters News Agency, took up my defense.

I continued my journalistic work after I was released. I was arrested again one evening in December 1992. I was taken to the main prison in Gaza City and put in a large cell together with fourteen other men. These men were all top leaders of the Hamas and the Islamic Jihad movement. Our arrest followed the kidnapping and murder of an Israeli border policeman, Nisim Toledano, by members of the Hamas military wing. We did not yet know the reason for our arrest. As it later turned out, we were supposed to be part of the large group of Hamas activists who were destined to be expelled from Palestine into Lebanon—in the operation that was later called the deportation of the 400 Hamas and Islamic Jihad leaders. That night we slept on the seven beds in two stories that were in the cell. We kept our spirits high by talking and joking most of the night. We were sure that the Israelis were planning to send us to Ketziot, the large prison camp in the Negev desert, where thousands of Palestinians who had been active in the intifada were incarcerated.

We were wrong. The next evening, the Israeli soldiers put all of us, together with many other fellow Palestinians whom they had arrested, on Israeli buses. Each Palestinian sat in a double seat alone, with his hands handcuffed behind his back and a sack on his head. Because of the sack, we could not see, but we sensed that the windows of the bus were open, and it was very cold. Israeli soldiers stood and sat in the bus and guarded us. The buses drove and drove for many hours; most of the night passed and we had not reached our destination. We slowly understood that we were probably not going to the Ketziot prison camp, which is at most a three-hour drive from Gaza City. The buses finally stopped and waited.

Suddenly, as we stood waiting, an Israeli soldier ascended our bus and called my name. I answered: Yes. He told me to come with him and pulled me out of the bus. I left the bus and followed him. Without explaining anything, he led me to a small, Renault army pickup. Soldiers put me in the back of the pickup. Two soldiers got in the front and two guarded me. Those in front started driving the car. I was still handcuffed and had a sack on my head. At first, I thought that the Israelis were planning to kill me. But after a while I understood that they were taking me somewhere. Finally, after a very long ride, we reached Gaza City and drove to Gaza Central Jail. I was taken out of the car and returned to a cell.

Later I was taken to the second floor of the jail, which Palestinians call the slaughterhouse, for interrogation. But the Israeli interrogators had nothing to ask me. The Shabak officer, Abu Karim, who had been responsible for interrogating me during my former jailing, was in charge.

After a while he said, "I have nothing against you. We put you in the bus for deportation by mistake."

"Deportation? Where to?" I asked.

"To Lebanon."

"How could you say that you put me on the bus by mistake when you saw me in the cell a day before the deportation?" I questioned him.

He did not answer. "Do you mean to say that the people who were with me in the cell are now in Lebanon?" I asked again.

"Yes," he answered and told the soldiers to return me to the cell.

Two days later I was released. It was then that I learned that my employers from *The New York Times*, Reuters News Agency, and many foreign journalists had intervened on my behalf. My Israeli friends Rivca and Haim Gordon had also put pressure on Israeli Knesset members to have me released. They all had demanded that the Israeli army release me immediately. With my release, I became a sort of celebrity; many journalists wanted to interview me. That soon passed and I returned to my journalistic work.

I have very few Israeli friends. My friendship with Rivca and Haim Gordon and their son, Neve, is exceptional. Perhaps here is the place to explain the difficulties that we Palestinians face when we consider the possibility of establishing friendships with Israelis. These considerations are all linked to the Israeli occupation and its ways of ruining our daily life and suppressing our freedom.

When meeting an Israeli, the Palestinian will frequently fear that the new Israeli acquaintance may attempt to recruit him or her to work for the Israeli security service, the Shabak. All Palestinians know that the Israeli armed forces are always seeking additional collaborators. We also know that the Shabak often employs Israeli civilians to help them recruit new Palestinian collaborators. This search for collaborators creates an atmosphere of mistrust which probably serves the goals of the Shabak. One consequence of this mistrust is that many Palestinians are hesitant about becoming friendly with Israelis. These Palestinians are afraid that they might be branded as supporters of the oppressive Israeli regime or as collaborators.

The growth of friendship between Rivca and Haim Gordon and myself during the intifada was therefore quite exceptional. I soon recognized that their goal was to support the just struggle of the Palestinian people. I felt that there was no reason to be suspicious of their brave activities. In their struggle for our human rights, Rivca and Haim also met with leaders of all factions of the Palestinian people, moderates and extremists. During the hundreds of times that they visited the Gaza Strip during the intifada and afterward, they always endeavored to help any Palestinian whose human rights were abused by the Israeli authorities. I knew that any Palestinian could call them on the phone any time, day or night, and they would try to help. My recognition of the significance of their activities helped me to establish our friendship.

I want to mention a few recent events in which I participated and which influenced my life and understanding of the current situation in the Gaza Strip— a very sad situation in which we Palestinians find ourselves. On May 18, 1994, the first units of the Palestinian armed forces entered the Gaza Strip. I covered the story of their entrance for the news agencies with whom I was in contact: BBC, CBS News, the *New York Times*, Reuters News Agency, and others. But that evening, the Palestinian police arrested my brother Amer, who was working with me that day as a cameraman for CBS News. The reason given for his arrest was that he had photographed and filmed Palestinian policemen without permission. I was shocked and bewildered. Suddenly I grasped that we Palestinians in the Gaza Strip had merely changed one oppressive ruler for another.

A few weeks later, I was arrested by the Palestinian police. After six days, I was released. No reason was given for my arrest, nor was I charged with any misconduct. A few weeks passed, and again I was arrested by the Palestinian police. It soon became clear to me that I was being arrested because my office in Gaza City had reported to the international press agencies with whom I was working news items about attacks against Israeli targets by Palestinian activists. My two arrests in 1994 were ordered by President Yasser Arafat. Probably, President Arafat was embarrassed by the news items that I conveyed to the outside world concerning what was happening within the Gaza Strip. He decided to punish me.

My arrests by the Palestinian police were also a result of my success as a journalist. The news office that I had opened in Gaza City, in which I was the sole representative of Reuters News Agency, the *New York Times*, CBS News, BBC, and other news agencies in Europe and the Far East, had become very well known. All the Palestinian organizations would send me their announcements and their press releases, hoping that my office would convey their statements to the international media.

A few days after my second arrest, Zahra attended a meeting in which she met Yasser Arafat. At that meeting, Zahra identified herself as my wife; she then asked Arafat why I was in jail. Arafat said that I was problematic. He added that Reuters News Agency had reported some lies about what was happening in the Gaza Strip, and he held me accountable for those lies. Arafat promised Zahra that I would be released by the following Monday, but I was not released. By chance, a few days later Arafat went to pray in Abbas mosque, which is next to the police station where I was being held prisoner. I was allowed out of the police station when I said that I, too, was going to pray. In the mosque, I approached President Arafat and asked him how long he would hold me prisoner. He slowly turned to me, looked me over, and told me to go home—which I gladly did.

At 3:00 one morning in April 1995, a small group of Palestinian policemen came to the group of apartments that I shared with my brothers to arrest me again. I decided to hide and fled to the roof. Fortunately, it was a very dark night, and I was wearing a pair of dark pajamas which could not be seen in the darkness. I was not caught, but the policemen harassed my family, and my mother wept. They also beat my brothers severely; one of my brothers was knocked unconscious.

In the morning I phoned the office of General Nasser Yusef, who is formally the chief of staff of the Palestinian armed forces. I asked him why Palestinian policemen had come to arrest me. He said that he had no knowledge of the incident. These arrests, however, led me to decide to be careful and frequently discuss my work as a journalist with representatives of the Palestinian Authority.

The discussions did not help me much. As the years passed, my daily work as a journalist was slowly and efficiently blocked by the Israeli armed forces and also by the Palestinian Authority. Being blocked as a journalist caused me great frustration, since I knew that there were important truths about the Gaza Strip to convey to the world and that I was capable of conveying these truths. It was suggested that I compromise the truth, but I firmly refused. After four years of great frustration in my journalistic work, I decided to take a respite from journalism and leave the Gaza Strip for a few years.

Personally, today I feel uncomfortable when I meet most Israelis and many Jews. Most Israelis, including many of those whom I met while they were serving in the army, know very well the extent and the depth of the suffering of the Palestinian people. They also know that decades of Israeli oppression and exploitation are the reason for this great suffering. Yet, these Israelis continue to support the unjust occupation of our lands and the blatant denial of our personal and political freedom.

I should perhaps add that I am not very optimistic about the future of the Palestinian people under the rule of what we currently call the Palestinian Authority. The Palestinian Authority is quite undemocratic, as their way of relating to my journalistic activities reveals. Hence, today our political freedom is very limited. I was oppressed by both the Israeli military and later by certain officials in the Palestinian Authority. Yet, the wicked oppression of the Israeli military was definitely what caused the greatest pain and frustration.

Finally, I want to state a few obvious truths. The Israeli oppression is blatant evil, and as such destroys our freedom. Hence, the future of the Palestinian people hardly looks encouraging. I fear that much blood will be shed until the Israeli leaders make the brave decision to terminate their occupation of Palestinian land and end their military rule of the Palestinian people. I believe that President Yasser Arafat is the best Palestinian leader with whom Israelis can sign a peace treaty. He is the only leader whom the overwhelming majority of Palestinians perceive and accept as a genuine, brave peacemaker.

Chapter 8

Mahmoud Zahar

By the blessing of Allah, I was born in the Zaitoon quarter of Gaza City on May 6, 1945. In 1947, together with my mother, who was my father's third wife, we moved to Ismailia, a city located on the Suez Canal in Egypt. I grew up in Egypt until 1958.

My father's first wife was his cousin. Islam allows marriage of cousins. She died from an unknown disease six months after their marriage. In the early 1930s, he married a second woman, who was many years older than he and had a child from a previous marriage. They had three children. After 1939, however, this woman could no longer give birth. My father, who was an orphan, and was an only child after his sister died at age of six months, wanted additional children. At the advice of a neighbor, he traveled to Egypt in 1943 and met there a relative of this neighbor. After a short traditional courtship, my father married her. He returned with my mother to Gaza City, where I was born. In the next few years, my mother gave birth to three additional sons and a daughter.

In 1947, my father no longer found work as a mechanic of tractors and other vehicles in the Gaza Strip area. After the end of World War II, the British army left the immediate area of the Gaza Strip and there was less need for mechanics. My father decided to move to Ismailia in Egypt, where my mother's family resided in the Shouhada quarter. Shouhada is the Arabic word for "martyrs." My father's second wife preferred to remain in Gaza City and asked for a divorce, which she received. I grew up in Ismailia, where my father worked as a mechanic. My uncles and aunts and my maternal grandmother lived there, so I did not feel that I was an alien. My family was quite well-off economically until the 1956 war, when Egypt was attacked by the British, French, and Israeli armies. Like many others who lived in the area of the Suez Canal, which became a war zone, we were forced to flee Ismailia into the Egyptian countryside.

After the war, my father could not find work. He tried to find work in Saudia Arabia but became ill there, and in 1958, we returned to Gaza City.

Growing up in Ismailia until the age of twelve, I remember being a good pupil in school. I also remember playing football (soccer) with other children in the streets; I was quite a good player. It was quite common to play football in the street; many talented Egyptian football players, who attained fame in later years, began by playing in the streets. One of these players was an uncle of mine, who later played on the Egyptian team in the African football games, and who, as a youth, learned to play football in the streets.

During the last years that we resided in Ismailia, I witnessed three incidents in which the British soldiers who ruled the Suez Canal area clashed with the Egyptian population. In two of the incidents, an unarmed and poor Egyptian was arbitrarily killed by British soldiers. In a third incident, a British soldier was killed by members of the Moslem Brothers, an influential Islamic movement in Egypt at that time. I sensed that many people in Ismailia, among them many of my school friends, sympathized with the military struggle of the Moslem Brothers against the British army.

Upon our return to the Gaza Strip, which until 1967 was under the military rule of Egypt, I entered the Zaitoon school. I completed primary school with excellent grades. In secondary school, I was first in my class in academic studies and was also a very good football player. In 1962, I was recognized as the best student in the Gaza Strip and also as captain of the football team. I was only seventeen years old. I continued to excel in my studies, including drawing. For my secondary studies, I went to Palestine High School and completed my secondary studies in 1965 with excellent grades. My grades were high enough to allow me to enter the college of medicine at Ein Shams University in Cairo. At that time, studying at Egyptian universities was tuition-free for both Egyptian and Palestinian students.

Before leaving the Gaza Strip to study in Cairo, I was required by the Liberation Army of the Palestinians to participate in a month of military training in the Gaza Strip. I learned to use a rifle and a machine gun, fire five hundred rounds, and throw grenades. In October 1965, after the training, I traveled to Cairo and commenced my studies. The first year at the university was called preparatory medicine, and I completed it with excellent grades. The second year of my studies, which commenced in January 1967, was in the medical school. That period of my life was dedicated to intensive study, with almost no political involvement. My only goals during those years were to receive high grades, to graduate, and to become a medical doctor. I clearly remember that many of my student friends who were from the Gaza Strip had similar goals.

In June 1967, the war between Israel and Egypt broke out, and Israel swiftly captured the Gaza Strip and the Sinai Peninsula. It was a shock for us, since we students had participated in military training and were confident of an Arab victory. When the battle started, we were sure that Jaffa and Haifa would soon be in Arab hands. However, from the BBC radio broadcasts, we soon learned that the Egyptian air force had been demolished and that the Egyptian army had retreated. In a few days, we grasped that the Gaza Strip was now in the hands of the Israeli army, as was the entire Sinai Peninsula. We recognized the extent of the Egyptian defeat. One night when there was an air raid on Cairo, I went out into the street to watch the anti-aircraft guns firing at the Israeli planes. Standing there alone, I did not feel at all frightened; I merely wanted to witness the battle.

With the Egyptian military defeat, my personal situation as a Palestinian student in Cairo became very problematic. I was stranded in Egypt without a source of income. My family in Gaza City had supported me during my studies. As a result of the Israeli victory and Israel's occupation of the Gaza Strip and the Sinai Peninsula, all direct links with my family were cut. At that moment, I did have nine Egyptian pounds, which my father had sent me so that I could buy a suit. That money could support me for a while. I was living in a small apartment with other Palestinian students. Our landlord, who was an uneducated but humane man, understood our dire situation and refused to evict us. He told us that we could stay in the apartment and pay when we obtained funds. In general, despite the defeat and its many sad consequences, I felt that the Egyptian people were not spiritually broken.

My personal financial situation as a medical student became easier when the Arab League decided to give each Palestinian student studying in Egypt nine Egyptian pounds a month for living expenses. That sum was sufficient for me to live frugally while I continued my studies. I successfully completed my medical studies in 1971. During my four years of studies, I was unable to return to the Gaza Strip. The reason was that I had left the Gaza Strip before the June 1967 war. Consequently, the Israeli authorities did not recognize me as a resident of the Gaza Strip. When I graduated in June 1971 and the stipend from the Arab League ended, my brother Hussein, who was working in Saudi Arabia, started sending me money so that I could stay in Egypt and get some experience as a medical doctor. In any event, I was not allowed to return to the Gaza Strip.

I resided and practiced medicine as a general practitioner in Egypt for more than a year after becoming a doctor. In the meantime, the Israeli authorities recognized that there was an acute shortage of medical doctors in the Gaza Strip. There was no medical school in the Gaza Strip or on the West Bank. In negotiations with Egypt through the Red Cross, the Israeli authorities arranged for the return to the Gaza Strip of forty-two young Palestinian medical doctors who had lived in the Gaza Strip and had completed their studies in Egypt. Those doctors who agreed to return to Gaza were promised identity cards, which the Israelis issued for the Palestinians residing in the Occupied Territories. Since I had previously contacted the Red Cross and asked them to help me return to the Gaza Strip, I was included among the forty-two returning medical doctors. We were divided into two groups. On October 18, 1972, the first group of doctors, to which I belonged, returned to the Gaza Strip, and on the morrow we received our Israeli identity cards. Three days later we started to work at Shiffa Hospital, which is the major hospital in the Gaza Strip. The second group of doctors returned in February 1973.

With my return, I grasped that it was a most important mission to improve the standard of health in the Gaza Strip. The few doctors who were practicing in the Gaza Strip were overburdened; we, the new young doctors, believed that we could help them and substantially improve the level of medical services. When I arrived in Gaza City, my only experience had been that of a general practitioner. In my work at Shiffa Hospital, I learned and practiced in various departments. For two months I worked in the department of births, helping in the delivery of babies; after that I worked in surgery. I thus gained experience and knowledge.

In order to improve the medical awareness of our fellow Palestinians, in the first months of 1973, five of us new doctors decided to write a book about first aid which would serve as a guide for the general public. We sought a publisher but did not find one. Finally, the Palestinian Red Crescent Society, under the leadership of Dr. Haidar Abdul Shafi, published the book. We also wanted the publication of the book to be linked to an educational program that stressed first aid. But both the Israeli authorities and UNRWA refused to sponsor such an educational program. Finally, the Red Crescent Society also sponsored the educational program, and we held a number of courses on first aid in the Red Crescent Society building and in other locations. My activities during that period concentrated on raising awareness of my fellow Palestinians as to the ways to improve and sustain health among our people.

In February 1974, the small Nasser Hospital in the city of Khan Yunis was reopened, after having been closed for a long time. In the meantime, I had been very active at Shiffa Hospital in requesting a raise in our salaries. The health authority, which was headed by an Israeli officer who had a few Palestinian subordinates, was not pleased with these activities; hence, the health authority transferred me to the reopened hospital in Khan Yunis, which was located twenty miles away from my home. During the first few months we found that much work had been delayed when the hospital was closed. Consequently, we worked many hours trying to help the people. I rarely went home to Gaza City. During that period, I was also working as a volunteer at the Al-Kuran dispensary, which was sponsored by the Red Crescent Society.

In March 1974, the value of our salaries went down, due to a rapid inflation in prices. We demanded an increase in salaries, but the health authority, headed by the Israeli army officers, rejected our demand. Dr. Fouad Zaqout and I represented the medical doctors at Khan Yunis Hospital. We met with the doctors in Gaza City and demanded that all doctors in the Gaza Strip declare a strike. We met on a Thursday and presented a motion to notify the health authority that a strike would begin the following Sunday. There were doctors working in Gaza City who tried to convince their colleagues not to strike. Finally, Fouad and I notified our colleagues at the meeting that if they refused to decide upon a strike of all the doctors in the Gaza Strip, only the doctors in Khan Yunis would strike. We told them that they had the right to join us or not to join us. We then got up and left the meeting.

At that point, some of the doctors from Gaza City followed us and requested that we not leave the meeting. After much discussion outside the meeting hall, we returned to the meeting. At the reconvened meeting, everyone finally decided to support our motion, and the health authority was notified that unless our demands for a fair salary were met, there would be a strike of all the medical doctors in the Gaza Strip the following Sunday. In response, the Israeli authorities immediately summoned five of our representatives for a meeting with them. After much discussion, the Israelis made the neccessary concessions to cancel the strike. Among their concessions were the decision to raise our salary to a tolerable living standard and the decision to link it to the value of the dollar. When the medical doctors in the Gaza Strip saw the favorable change in their salary, they remembered that Fouad and I had firmly stood up for their just cause and had supported their needs.

In October 1974, together with a small group of doctors from the Gaza Strip, I returned to Egypt to specialize in surgery. The Red Cross arranged for our travel, but the expenses were paid by each of the doctors. Some of my colleagues stayed for only one year and returned to Gaza with diplomas in their areas of specialization. I decided to stay two years and completed a master's degree. I returned to the Gaza Strip in early 1977. Since the Red Cross no longer dealt with transferring doctors from Egypt to the Gaza Strip, I flew to Amman in Jordan; from there I returned on the morrow to Gaza City via the bridge on the Jordan River and through the West Bank and Israel. I resumed my work at the hospital in Khan Yunis.

It was quite uncommon for a man of my age, thirty-two years old in 1977, to be still unmarried. In January 1978, I married Samira Khamis Agha, a teacher from Gaza City. On December 1, 1978, my first daughter, Reem, was born. This year, 2000, Reem will receive her bachelor's degree in engineering. I have six children. My oldest son Khaled, who was born a year after Reem, has finished his studies as an accountant. My youngest son, Husam, is still in primary school.

Upon my return to Gaza in 1977, I gave the local doctors a series of lectures about general surgery. My first public activities after my return were related to renewing the activities of the society of medical workers. The society included medical doctors, pharmacists, dentists, and veterinarians. The first elections for the governing board of the medical society took place in January 1978, and I was elected to be a member of the board. This seemed appropriate since I was responsible for founding the Khan Yunis branch of the society and was in charge of the administration of that branch. After a year, however, a new governing board was elected. The reason was that some people complained that the bad relations between the previous governing board of the medical society and the Israeli health authority had hindered the society. They convinced the members to elect a new governing board. But the members soon felt that this board was not good, and in the elections of 1980 they elected most of the members of the previous board of directors to govern the society. Dr. Sayed Bakr was chosen to be president of the society and I was chosen to be vice president. Dr. Sayed was often absent due to his frequent travels, and I chaired the meetings. This role gave me much experience.

In the winter of 1982, at the age of thirty-six, I was chosen to be the president of the medical society of the Gaza Strip. One reason for that choice was that I campaigned as an independent candidate. Almost half of the members of the medical society were leftists, and almost all of the other half of the members were affiliated with the Fatah or the Islamic Bloc, which voted together against the leftists. I was chosen by agreement, since both factions recognized that no side could win, and, being independent, I threatened neither side. It was very uncommon for someone at my age to be elected to such a position.

In 1981, before being elected to the position of president of the medical society, I participated, together with a group of colleagues, in formally establishing the Islamic University in Gaza City. In 1980, we had already set up various committees to establish the university. I became a member of the founding board of the Islamic University. But in the early 1980s and especially after 1982, with my election as president of the medical society, my major responsibilities were linked to the medical society. I was then working in Shiffa Hospital in Gaza City.

In 1981, the situation concerning medical doctors had changed. There were 120 new Palestinian medical doctors in the Gaza Strip, all of whom had recently graduated from universities abroad. The problem was that almost none of them could find a job. Already in 1980, the governing board of the medical society believed that finding professional positions for these doctors could help improve the overall health situation in the Gaza Strip. The elected officials of the society, including myself, attempted to convince various official and volunteer organizations in the Gaza Strip to find positions in which to employ these doctors in their organizations. We also asked some organizations to employ these doctors for free but pay them an expense allowance. We were only partially successful in these endeavors.

In October 1981, the problem of the unemployed medical doctors was partially solved by our enlisting help from our fellow Arab medical doctors from different Arab countries. As a member of a group of twenty-three doctors from the Gaza Strip, I attended an Arab medical congress that was held in Amman, Jordan. It was the first time that a delegation of Palestinian medical doctors had attended a medical congress, and we were very warmly received by the official hosts of the congress and all the other delegations. We actively participated in lectures on academic and professional medical topics with Arab doctors from the other delegations. In the professional meetings, we brought up two issues: the problem of the medical doctors in the Gaza Strip who were unemployed and the need for some of our doctors to specialize in various medical areas.

Both problems were solved at that congress. Scholarships were arranged for Palestinian doctors who wished to specialize in a specific medical field. In addition, a fund was set up that would award 100 dinars a month (about $125) to each unemployed medical doctor in the Gaza Strip who worked professionally as a volunteer at an organization that helped people in the Gaza Strip. It was understood that if the doctor received another fifty dinars a month from the organization in which he volunteered, he would have enough money to live with dignity.

During the early 1980s, Palestinian organizations began to be recognized in various parts in the world. For instance, in 1980, we set up a sports committee that was affiliated with the Islamic University which we were planning to establish. After that, we arranged for the sports committee to receive a formal invitation to attend the 1980 Olympic Games that were held in Moscow. Despite the formal invitation, the Israeli authorities did not give the Palestinian committee permission to attend the Olympic Games. The Israelis often tried to sever our relations with other organizations in the world.

During my tenure as vice president and president of the medical society, the building that we rented became a center of social activities and sports for our members. We had a football team, and we held courses in chess and billiards. We showed films that were appropriate for all members of the family, and our members attended symposiums in Gaza City and abroad. Members of our medical society came to our building regularly, and often brought friends from other professional associations. Our activities were professional and social; they were not political—not yet. We also endeavored to reestablish links between professional people in the Gaza Strip and their peers in the Arab world; these links had hardly existed between 1967 and 1981.

Our first political clash with the Israeli military authorities that ruled the Gaza Strip came about with the establishing of the value added tax in Israel in the early 1980s. The Israeli military authorities decided that, as in Israel, businesses and residents of the Gaza Strip must also pay this tax. The decision was made by the Israeli military without consulting representatives of the Palestinian people and despite the fact that the income of the residents of the Gaza Strip was a fraction of the income of the citizens of Israel. Value added tax was an addition of more than 10 percent to the income tax that we Palestinians already paid to the Israeli occupying power. We medical doctors who were members of the medical society refused to pay this tax. We held that we were living in an occupied zone and were members of a politically oppressed people, and our Israeli oppressors had decided to tax us arbitrarily.

The response of the Israeli authorities came on Wednesday, November 28, 1982. Accompanied by Israeli soldiers, officials of the Israeli military tax authority for the Gaza Strip raided a number of private clinics and homes of medical doctors in the Gaza Strip. During the raid they searched the clinic and the home of each doctor and confiscated all the money that they found, including the money that was found in the doctor's wallet. They also arrested all the medical doctors whose clinics and homes were being searched. I was notified of this raid and immediately came to Shiffa Hospital. When I arrived, I discovered that almost all the members of the administrative board of the hospital and of the governing board of the medical society had been arrested. I notified everyone that on the morrow we would hold a meeting of all the doctors who were concerned by the actions of the Israeli authorities toward the medical doctors in the Gaza Strip. I announced that the meeting would be held in the office of the director of Shiffa Hospital.

On the morrow, a large number of medical doctors attended the meeting, which I chaired. We decided on three demands that we would submit to the Israeli military authorities. First, we demanded the immediate release of the arrested medical doctors and a halt to all the actions against medical doctors by the Israeli tax authorities. Our second demand was that the authorities promise to improve the medical services for the population of the Gaza Strip. Our third demand was that the authorities abolish the value added tax that had been unjustly imposed upon the people of the Gaza Strip. The first demand was linked to the medical society. The second and the third demands were for the entire population of the Gaza Strip and constituted an act of resistence to the cruelties of the Israeli occupation.

About 100 medical doctors participated in the consultations that led to formulating these demands. Many of these doctors were at the meeting that we held at Shiffa Hospital. We all decided to hold a strike until our demands were met. I believe that our decision to strike showed the Israeli authorities that Palestinian resistance to their cruel regime had not been broken. I should add that we received no instructions concerning our decision to resist the acts of the Israeli authorities—neither from people inside the Gaza Strip nor from the leadership of the various resistance movements outside Palestine that were struggling for liberation of our people.

The strike began immediately. We held a press conference and announced our demands and our decision to strike. After the conference, all the doctors at Shiffa Hospital and the medical clinics in Gaza City abandoned their posts and moved to the premises of the medical society, and there held a sit-in strike. We arranged for a small number of doctors to continue to work in the emergency, delivery, and children's wards of the hospitals in the Gaza Strip. We then called on all doctors at private clinics and all pharmacists to close their clinics and pharmacies and join us in the sit-in strike at the medical society. The response was remarkable; everyone joined us.

All the pharmacists in the Gaza Strip locked their pharmacies and joined us in the sit-in strike. They refused to open their shops, even under threat from the Israeli military authorities. In response, soldiers from the Israeli army broke down the doors of some of the pharmacies. Still, the pharmacists refused to return to their shops. The Israeli army then arrested all the phamacists in Gaza City for whole days, releasing them only at night. While this was happening, merchants from shops close to the pharmacies guarded the pharmacies and arranged for new doors to be built to replace the doors that the Israeli army had demolished. Through such actions, the strike gained popularity among our people; many people from Gaza City came to where the sit-in strike was held in order to express support and show solidarity.

Our strike lasted twenty-one days. During those days we received expressions of support from all the professional organizations in the Gaza Strip. We also received visits, telegrams, and other expressions of support from individuals and from organizations in the West Bank. We also organized, under the auspices of the medical society, a meeting of all the leaders of the ten professional associations in the Gaza Strip, such as the association of engineers and that of lawyers. Together we organized a general strike in the markets of the Gaza Strip on the next Saturday; it was the Saturday following the first week of December. The general strike was a complete success. On the day of the general strike, there were demonstrations against the Israeli occupation. During these demonstrations Israeli soldiers shot and killed a seventeen-year-old Palestinian, Mahmoud Abu Nahla.

The Israeli Civil Administration, which was the arm of the Israeli military that was in charge of daily life in the Gaza Strip, finally decided to negotiate with us. During the negotiations, they pretty much accepted our three demands. They released the medical doctors who had been arrested, and we paraded with them in an open car in the streets of Gaza City. In response to our second demand, a committee was formed to discuss the issue of taxes; we also noticed that after the strike, Israel changed its means of forcing people to pay taxes. In response to our third demand concerning health insurance, a joint committee of members of the medical society, the health department, and the Civil Administration was established. The role of the committee was to plan how to spend the money raised by the health insurance program to better the health conditions of the people of the Gaza Strip. There were disagreements in that committee, but that is another story.

On the first day of the strike, I was notified that I had been fired from my position as a doctor at Shiffa Hospital. The notification came from the hospital director, who was a Palestinian. He had received orders to dismiss me from the Israeli army officer who was director of the health department at the Israeli Civil Administration. The official reason for my being dismissed was that I had divulged facts concerning the nature of my work without receiving permission from the Civil Administration. The Civil Administration also announced that they would investigate me on this charge, but they never did. Everyone knew, however, that the real reason for my being fired was to punish me, because, as president of the medical society, I had led the strike against the Israeli military authorities. In their charges against me, the Civil Administration overlooked their own regulation that as president of the medical society, I did have permission to speak out. Hence, I appealed their decision to fire me. Discussions continued until May 1983, when I was finally dismissed.

I was married and had children to support but was suddenly without a regular salary. I had opened a private clinic in 1977. After my dismissal from

Shiffa Hospital, I spent more time there, working as a general practitioner who did minor surgeries. In addition, I continued to be president of the medical society until 1985, but I did not receive a salary for this work. In the 1985 elections of the medical society, I was not reelected to be president. A coalition of members of the Fatah and parties of the left chose a new board for the medical society, which chose a new president.

In 1982, the Islamic University engaged me to join a three-member committee that would perform a study on the nursing situation in the Gaza Strip. The choice of nurses who were certified to work in the Gaza Strip and the qualifications required to be a nurse were at that time determined by the Israeli military authorities. The Israelis determined what happened at the governmental nursing college, which was the only nursing college in the Gaza Strip. We had grave doubts that the Israeli military authorities always acted on behalf of the Palestinian people in deciding who was to be appointed as a nurse. We believed that for the Israelis who were in charge, allegiance to their military authority was more important than academic qualifications and training in nursing. Hence, persons admitted to the nursing college and the graduates of the college were quite often not the best nurses. For some years, I had taught courses on medicine at the governmental college for nursing and had learned what was happening at that institution.

Because of this situation, we wanted to establish an independent college for nursing. The study that our committee performed was the first step in this direction. After the submission of our study, in 1983 the board of directors of the Islamic University decided to establish a college of nursing. However, the Israeli military authorities immediately rejected the university's request to establish an independent college of nursing. In early 1985, Dr. Muhammad Siam, the newly appointed president of the Islamic University, confronted the Israeli authorities and opened a college of nursing. I was appointed as one of the teachers. The Israeli military authorities were angry and notified Dr. Siam that if he did not close the college of nursing, they would close the entire Islamic University. But he refused to close the college. The Israeli military authorities responded by refusing to recognize the certificates awarded to students who graduated from the Islamic University, thus hindering those students' ability to obtain work. Finally, in the fall of 1985, the Israeli military authorities forcefully closed the college of nursing.

Another response of the Israeli military was to put pressure on the professors to leave the Islamic University. For instance, one day the Israeli military governor called me and threatened that I would be killed unless I changed my actions. I told him that I had no weapons or guards. A few days later when I left my house in the morning to go to my clinic, I found two Israeli army jeeps and a military car standing outside my door, blocking my car, which stood in front of the house.

I asked them, "What are you doing here?"

They answered, "Fulfilling the orders that we received."

I then asked them to allow me to drive my car to work, and they moved a bit to let my car out. I entered my car and drove to work. The Israeli military vehicles immediately accompanied me, supposedly in order to guard me. One army jeep drove in front of me and the two other military cars drove behind me.

From that day on, for forty-five days, wherever I went there was always one Israeli army car in front of me and two Israeli army cars following me. If I picked up my wife at work or drove my children to school or to friends' homes, the military vehicles always accompanied me. After a few weeks, Israeli soldiers confiscated my driving license. I rode to my office on my bicycle, accompanied by the Israeli military vehicles. By these actions the Israeli military were suggesting to the population of the Gaza Strip, who saw me always accompanied by army vehicles, that I was being guarded by the Israeli army. An uninformed person might have concluded that the Israeli soldiers were guarding me because I was working with the Israeli Shabak, the secret service, against the Palestinian cause. In short, by their constantly accompanying me with military vehicles, the Israelis were trying to brand me a traitor and a collaborator. Despite the tension that I felt from the first moment, I did not appeal to the Israelis and did not ask them to stop harassing me.

The Israeli authorities' attempt to discredit me failed miserably. People understood that if I had been a collaborator, I would not have had my driving license confiscated and would not have had to ride a bike to get to work. Children began throwing stones at the Israeli soldiers who waited near my clinic. In order to challenge the Israelis, people began coming deliberately to my clinic to talk to me and express their support. Some of these visitors, among them old women, even yelled at the Israelis and told them to stop harassing me. In any case, after forty-five days the Israeli military vehicles stopped accompanying me, and they sent a policeman to my home to return my driving license.

At the end of 1985, together with other supposedly prominent Palestinians, I was arrested for a week and held at the Shajaya police center. It had to do with internal political disputes among the Palestinians, between members of Islamic and leftist parties. Since I had always stressed my professional work, I was not part of this dispute.

After my arrest, however, in addition to my work at my private clinic, I began teaching at the Islamic University and became affiliated with the Islamic resistance movement called the Hamas. The English meaning of Hamas is "zealot". I soon became an influential member and a member of the steering committee of the leadership of the Hamas.

On November 9, 1987, there were incidents similar to the intifada at the Islamic University. Students threw rocks at the Israeli soldiers, and in response an Israeli army unit stormed the university, wounding eighty-three students and closing the university. On that day, we treated the wounded students inside the university in a special clinic that we quickly set up. We knew that anyone who was wounded in a clash with Israeli soldiers and reached a hospital was reported to the Israeli military authorities. He or she could then be arrested. For the same reasons, during the intifada that erupted in December 1987, we medical doctors who had private clinics opened them to the lightly wounded, whom we treated in our clinics free of charge. Thus, we helped many of the wounded evade arrest.

After the beginning of the intifada, probably due to my leading position in the Hamas movement, I was frequently summoned to the buildings where the Israeli military authorities had offices and interrogated there by their representatives. On March 28, 1988, I responded to one of these summons. I was led into a room and found myself face to face with Shimon Peres. He was then Israel's foreign minister in the national unity government under Prime Minister Yitzhak Shamir. Yitzchak Rabin was the defense minister. Sitting beside Peres was Major General Dan Shomron, the Israeli army chief of staff. Other Israeli civilians and military officers were in the room. Peres turned to me and said that as a doctor, and as an Islamic leader, I should be interested in preventing bloodshed. He spoke Hebrew, I spoke Arabic, and there was a translator. I cited a saying from the Prophet Muhammed and then explained to Mr. Peres that he represented an oppressing regime and that we would fight the oppression as Muhammed instructed us. With his hand, General Shomron indicated to others that I was insane, but Peres continued speaking to me.

Peres then told me that he had offered the Gaza Strip to Egypt and to the Kingdom of Jordan, but both had refused to become involved or to take over the area. He asked: What are your suggestions?

I replied that we Palestinians were unwilling to return to Jordanian or Egyptian rule. We demanded full independence for the Palestinian people. For the intifada to stop, Israel must announce its intention to return to the 1967 borders. The Occupied Territories should be transferred to a group of leaders who the Palestinian people agree are their leaders. There should then be elections in the Palestinian territories and the Palestinian people should choose their leaders without Israeli intervention. Finally, the full Israeli withdrawal should proceed quickly. Mr. Peres said that Israel could withdraw from the Gaza Strip immediately, but withdrawal from the West Bank would take six months. I asked him about Jerusalem, and he said that its status was negotiable. I remember telling him that if Israel agreed to withdraw immediately from Jerusalem, the withdrawal would open all channels for peace between our peoples. On the morrow, I reported the meeting and what had happened in it to the international news agencies.

In April 1988, together with three other Palestinians, I was invited to the building of the Civil Administration. The Palestinians were Mr. Zuhair Rayes from the Fatah, Dr. Riyad Al-Agha from the Fatah, and Dr. Ibrahim Yazouri from the Hamas. I also represented the Hamas. At the Civil Administration building we were told that it was necessary for us to go to Tel Aviv to meet Israel's defense minister, Yitzchak Rabin. They then put us in a car and drove us to Tel Aviv. At our meeting, Mr. Rabin immediately announced that he knew that there was a threat, originating from Dr. Riyad Al-Agha, that anyone who attempted to set up an alternative to the Palestine Liberation Organization (PLO) will be assassinated.

The alternative to which Mr. Rabin was referring was the Hamas, to which two of us belonged. We did not respond to this statement. We did present our beliefs about the goals of the intifada, and I pretty much repeated what I had told Mr. Peres. I also emphasized that we were not against Jews, but against Zionism and its occupation of a land belonging to Muslims. I also remember that Dr. Yazouri told him that his emphasis on holding on to occupied land during a period of intercontinental missiles was strategic madness.

More than a year later, on May 14 or 15, 1989, during a curfew in the Gaza Strip, I was again summoned to a meeting with Mr. Rabin. This time the Israelis summoned around fifteen Palestinian leaders from all major movements; we were all driven to Tel Aviv to meet Mr. Rabin. The views I expressed were similar to those I had expressed in the previous meeting and in the meeting with Mr. Peres. As you can note from our history, these views had little influence on the Israeli leaders.

On May 17, 1989, two days after my meeting with Mr. Rabin, together with around 2,500 Palestinians suspected of being affiliated with the Hamas, I was arrested by the Israeli army. The structure of the Hamas had been disclosed, and I had a leadership role in the movement, a role which I shall not discuss. I was interrogated for a month, but there was no evidence against me, something which surprised my interrogators. Still, my security detention was extended by the Israeli military for two months, and after that I was sentenced to administrative detention for an additional three months. Altogether, I was in jail for almost six months without being charged. I was released in October 1989.

The manner of arrest and the interrogations were brutal. The Israeli soldiers came at about 10:30 P.M. to arrest me. They tied a sack over my head, handcuffed me, and then pushed me into the back of a truck in which lay a heap of Palestinian male prisoners. In the back of the truck stood soldiers who continually beat us. Additional prisoners were added. When the truck finally entered Gaza Central Prison at 11:00 P.M., they sat us down in the yard of the prison, on the ground. Each of us sat there, handcuffed and with a sack over his head, for five hours, until 4:00 A.M. During these hours, Israeli soldiers guarded us and continued to beat us. Finally, we were transferred to Ansar II detention camp in Gaza City.

After two days at the detention camp, I was returned to Gaza Central Prison for interrogation. There, like many other prisoners, I was tortured for days on end. For instance, I was forced to sit for days on a chair with my head covered with a sack and my hands tied behind my back. While sitting there, soldiers who were passing would beat me. There was very little to eat, and it was hard to breathe because the sack was thick and wet. I fainted, and an Israeli nurse said that I was sick. But after a few hours, the torture continued; I was again tied in the chair with a sack over my head. During this ordeal, they allowed me to go to the toilet for only one minute during the entire day. Often the interrogators would beat me while trying to get me to admit to violently working against the Israeli occupying forces. One officer who interrogated me hit me in my larynx four consecutive times, and after that I had great difficulties swallowing for a month. The interrogators did not allow me to sleep for ten days. Finally, I was put in a cell where I could rest, but my cellmate was a Palestinian collaborator, who tried to get information out of me. After a few weeks of continual torture, the interrogators finally understood that there was no information to get out of me. I was then sentenced to administrative detention.

Upon my release from prison in October 1989, in addition to my daily medical work, I continued my leadership role in the Hamas. I was also recognized as one of the few unofficial spokespersons for the Hamas. The movement has never had an official spokesperson, an approach that allowed the movement to evade committing itself to a specific policy. Unofficial spokespersons could raise issues that the public would, hopefully, discuss. One of my earlier statements aroused anger among Israelis. In 1988, during one of my interviews on Israeli television, I announced that the Hamas wished to establish an Islamic state on the entire land of Palestine, which included the land currently occupied by the state of Israel. I added that until this goal was achieved, our struggle would continue.

The next major event linked to my political activities was my being deported in December 1992, together with around 415 Islamic activists. This occurred after the kidnapping and killing of an Israeli border policeman, Nissim Toledano, by Islamic activists. Close to midnight on Monday, December 14, the Israeli army arrested me and detained me in a cell in the central jail in Gaza City. The following morning I was put in a room with fifteen other prisoners, and we all understood that we were to be deported. The Israeli soldiers did not treat us violently. On Wednesday evening we were taken to a bus. Our hands were handcuffed behind our backs, our eyes were blindfolded, and our feet were tied with plastic thongs. The bus started driving and we were on it for thirty-six hours, driving and stopping. We did not know where we were going. It was raining, and the windows of the bus were purposely left open so that the rain came in, wetting us in the cold.

Finally, on Friday morning, we were taken off the bus and our blindfolds were removed. A $50 bill was put in each person's pocket; we grasped immediately that the $50 bill meant that we had been deported. We were then herded by Israeli soldiers onto the back of lorries that were waiting for us. Lebanese officers and soldiers, who were working with the Israeli army, were in charge of the lorries. A man who was there told us that we were in South Lebanon. Standing packed together in the back of seven lorries, we were driven about seven kilometers into Lebanon. The lorries halted and we were told to disembark. We refused. We explained our situation to the Lebanese officers and demanded that they return us to Israel and not take part in our deportation. After consultation, the Lebanese officers allowed the drivers to drive us back to the Israeli border. But before we were close to the border, Israeli soldiers opened fire from their side of the border, shooting around the lorries. The drivers turned back and we were forced to remain in South Lebanon.

Our immediate decision was to set up a community and a camp for all of us deported Palestinians on one of the hills of South Lebanon. We thus notified the world that our deportation by the Israeli occupation forces had been illegal and unjust. It was an unjust act of collective punishment. We decided not to abandon the camp until all of us were allowed to return to our homes in Palestine. We received tents and blankets from international aid organizations; food and other contributions came from Arab organizations and from simple people who wished to support us. We chose twenty-five people to be the general committee that would run the camp. I was a member of that committee. The general committee formed five subcommittees, such as the nutrition committee and the guarding committee, whose roles were to organize our daily life and to ensure that life in the camp ran smoothly.

I was appointed head of the media committee. The role of our committee was to alert the people of the world as to the illegality of Israel's deeds when it deported us. We wanted countries and organizations to put pressure on the Israeli government to allow us to return to our homes. As time passed, our lives became more organized. We documented what was happening in the camp and conveyed it to the world media. We also gathered information about what was happening in the world and passed on the information to all members of our community of deported Palestinians. Probably, as a result of the broad media coverage and the injustice done to us, many representatives of Arab countries and organizations, and quite a few visitors from other countries, reached our camp. My brother Fadel, who had been deported to Lebanon in 1990, came to visit me quite often, as did my mother, who had gone to visit Fadel and other members of Fadel's family who had joined him in exile.

We had a very large tent that served as a mosque. In that tent we also established and ran what we called our university; classes were held by the teachers and professors among us for all those who wished to learn. Another tent served as a clinic. Among the 415 Palestinians who were deported to Lebanon were seven medical doctors, four pharmacists, and four male nurses. Together we ran the clinic. Equipment and medicine were provided by human rights organizations and by many Palestinian and Lebanese factions. We took care of the immediate health problems of the deported Palestinians in our camp. Severe problems were referred to a hospital. Many Lebanese people from surrounding villages also came to our clinic if they had a health problem. We were happy to help them.

We succeeded in most of our goals. After a year of living in exile, the large majority of the Palestinians who had been deported by Israel in December 1992 were allowed to return to Palestine. Upon our return to Israel, we were all taken to a large jail camp in the desert, the Ketziot Camp, which was also called Ansar III Camp. We stayed there for four days and were interrogated. After four days we were brought back to the Gaza Strip and allowed to resume our life. That was quite a victory, and the celebrations in the Gaza Strip continued for a week. Large crowds came to the home of each one of the returned deportees in order to congratulate him and hear his story.

Although I did not support the Oslo Agreement, I am happy that the Palestinian Authority returned home and is no longer in exile. That is also the official position of the Hamas, which was against the Oslo Agreement. As one of the leaders of the Hamas movement, together with others, I wished to establish a dialogue with the leaders of the Palestinian Authority. But relations between the leadership of the Hamas and the Palestinian Authority did not develop in the direction of dialogue. The Palestinian Authority became angry when members of the Hamas movement caught, interrogated, and put to death two Palestinians from Gaza who confessed that they had collaborated with Israel. We leaders of the Hamas also angered the Palestinian Authority in other incidents, such as when members of Ez Adeen Al Qassam, which is an organization affiliated with the military wing of the Hamas, shot at Israeli settlers in the Gaza Strip.

One such incident of shooting at Israeli settlers by people affiliated with the Hamas occurred a month after Yasser Arafat arrived in the Gaza Strip. I was summoned to the police station and Muhammad Dahlan, head of the Palestinian security forces, was there waiting for me. When I arrived, he was speaking to Yasser Arafat on the telephone. Dahlan passed the telephone to me. I told Arafat that we believed that the only way to get the Israeli settlers to evacuate the Gaza Strip was to shoot at the settlers and the Israeli soldiers who guarded them. My views angered Arafat, and he notified me that my views were against the interests of the Palestinian people. After the telephone conversation, Dahlan told me that if we continued to initiate and support acts of violence against Israelis, the Palestinian Authority would have to act against us. He mentioned that the measures against us could include arrests. I rejected his threats and our meeting ended on a note of uresolved tension.

In March 1995, Yasser Arafat accepted an invitation from the president of the Islamic University, whose administration includes leaders and supporters of the Hamas. He spoke to the deans and a group of professors and administrators. That was the first time that I met Arafat. At that meeting, I was the only participant who challenged his views and criticized the Oslo Agreement. I expressed the view that he did not have to accept the Israeli conditions spelled out in the Oslo Agreement. I mentioned that we residents of the Occupied Territories often knew the situation better than the leadership outside the territories, and that he gave up much too much when he signed the Oslo Agreement. Arafat was quite annoyed with my criticism, but it did not lead to a confrontation.

At the end of May 1995, officers of the Palestinian police arrested me. The official reason was a leaflet, supposedly distributed by the Hamas, accusing members of the Palestinian Authority, among them Musa Arafat, of espionage against the Palestinian people. Musa Arafat is a close relative of Yasser Arafat; he came to the Gaza Strip in 1994 and became commander of the military intelligence, which is part of the police force. We leaders of the Hamas denied publishing this leaflet, but members of our leadership were arrested. I was in jail for three and a half months—fifty days in solitary confinement and fifty-five days in a cell with two other people. During this period my head was shaved, I was not allowed to receive visits, and I was not allowed to walk each day in the sun. During the first twenty-four hours of my incarceration I was beaten four times while my hands and legs were tied and a sack covered my head and eyes. The so-called interrogators broke five bones in my arms and feet, and I was taken to the hospital and registered as a prisoner, without my name being disclosed.

I firmly believe that the cruel deeds performed against me and others by the Palestinian Authority were not done for the good of the Palestinian people. They were a result of a faulty and unjust policy initiated and fulfilled by leaders of the Palestinian Authority. Much later I learned that the military wing of the Hamas wanted to retaliate against the Palestinian Authority for our being imprisoned. Two men from Jebalia Refugee Camp, who were members of our military wing, tried to blow up Musa Arafat and his intelligence organization. They prepared eighty-kilogram bombs for this mission and made two attempts. They failed, because twice the detonators did not work. I thank God for this failure. I have no doubt that such a violent deed would have led to disturbances within Palestinian society with terrible results for all Palestinians.

The overall aim of the Hamas movement, like other Islamic movements in the world, is to establish an Islamic regime that would rule over one great Islamic State. Such a regime existed 1,400 years ago, under the khalifate. It had districts and provinces, but they were all part of one great Islamic State. Today, such a state, I believe, should include all the Islamic countries, from Turkey to Morocco and beyond. In this state, Islamic principles would be the rule of law. As a result of these views, we do not accept the borders between the Arab states that were set down after World War I. We do not accept nationalities as determining borders.

We also do not accept the idea of a Palestinian State that is an entity which is separate from a great Islamic State. Even if this entity is established on Palestinian soil, we believe that in the future it should be part of a great Islamic State. Of course, we are ready to have a Palestinian State established, and we join in fighting for a free Palestinian State. But our demand is that the Palestinian State should be a first step in redeeming all Palestinian land, including the land that is now the State of Israel, and all that land should ultimately be part of an Islamic State.

Hamas, however, is not only a military movement. It is true that we continue to be active militarily against the Israeli occupation. But it is also true that we work in many social and political realms. We want to change the pattern of life in our society and alter the social behavior of our people so that they will live in accordance with Islamic principles. We fight against corruption, bribery, and favoritism in Palestinian life, both on the national and the municipal levels. We

want social life and the systems within which we live to be fair. We believe that
since we work for true faith, history is on our side and the balance of power will
not always favor the enemies of Islam.

Here are some additional facts. From its inception, the Hamas concentrated
on educating youth. Of course, we educated them to forcefully resist the brutal
Israeli occupation. But we also educated them to fight corruption within the
Palestinian State. The military wing affiliated with the Hamas movement has
been less active in the military field lately because of the cooperation between
the Israelis and the Palestinian Authority. This cooperation is supported by the
intelligence organizations of the United States and of members of the European
Union. These united forces of intelligence organizations help Israel and the
Palestinian Authority to curb our activities. I must admit that they partially
succeeded in reducing the activities of the military wing affiliated with the
Hamas.

I have grave doubts that the Hamas movement will ever give up the military
option. Hamas may support a political party and participate in political activity,
but the resistence program will always be a sword in its hands. It will choose the
right time to use that sword.

Hamas is a worldwide movement of the Palestinian people who support the
Islamic goals that I described. It has supporters in many Arab countries and has
good relations with the Arab regimes. We concentrate our efforts on freeing
Palestine and Jerusalem, and are not involved in the internal regimes of those
countries in which we work. A testimony to the good relations that we have
with other Arab regimes was the recent trip of Sheikh Ahmed Yassin, the
founder and leader of the Hamas, to many Arab countries. He was welcomed by
leaders in all of these countries and obtained much political and financial support for the Hamas.

The funding for the Hamas comes solely from charitable contributions. We
have not received governmental contributions from Arab regimes, but we do
not reject the possibility that governments may contribute funds to our movement. Such a contribution must be given with the understanding that there are
no strings attached to the receipt of the funds from a specific government. The
funds that we receive are used to support families of martyrs and of Palestinian
prisoners in Israeli jails, and also to help rehabilitate those Palestinians who
were wounded in the struggle against Israeli occupation. We also use the funds
for our educational and religious activities.

The decision-making process within the Hamas is by consultation among all
active leaders of the Hamas, including leaders of our movement who reside
outside of Palestine. Hamas has its own parliament which participates in the
decision-making process.

Part 3

Beyond Intifada

Chapter 9

The New Intifada and Israel's War Crimes

As mentioned in the introduction, when this book was conceived, we authors believed that the freedom fighters whose narratives we have presented had partially achieved their goal. We believed that the peace process which had commenced in 1993 would, at least partially, award the Palestinian people a state where they could live in freedom. We were wrong. As this book goes to press, the Palestinian people still do not have a state of their own. Indeed, some Palestinian spokespersons have noted that the Palestinian people are the last nation on the face of the earth that is living under military occupation.

What happened in the short period between the days that this book was conceived and researched and the months that it was written and edited into book form? The answer: Intifadet El Aqsa!

Let us recall the more recent events that led to this second Palestinian rebellion. Intifadet El Aqsa, which erupted on September 28, 2000, was ignited by the visit of Ariel Sharon, then leader of the Israeli opposition party Likud, to the Islamic third most holy shrine of El Aqsa, the Temple Mount. Israel's prime minister, Ehud Barak, leader of the Labor Party, allowed Sharon to organize and conduct this visit despite the pleadings of Yasser Arafat, who sensed that it might lead to chaos. On this visit, 1,000 Israeli policemen accompanied Sharon. Many Muslims throughout the world considered this visit to be an act of aggression, an attempt to show that their holy shrine could be taken over by brute force.

As already intimated, Palestinian spokespersons have repeatedly stated that the reasons for the recent Palestinian rebellion are much broader and deeper than Sharon's unwarranted, aggressive visit to the Temple Mount. As the narratives and the other chapters of this book reveal, in the background of this rebellion is Israel's three and a half decades of military rule of the Palestinian people. Probably the major recent reason for the eruption of Intifadet El Aqsa is Israel's continual refusal to abide by the Oslo Agreement that it signed in 1993—an agreement that led to the termination of the first intifada.

Put differently, Palestinians, from President Arafat down to the laborer in the field, state that Israel's continual military oppression and its deceit of the Palestinian people, especially in relation to the fulfillment of the peace accords that it signed in 1993, slowly created a situation that was unbearable. They add: When Israeli deeds trampled on our trust and continually denied us freedom, we Palestinians felt that our dignity had been soiled. Unfortunately, they add, this oppression and deceit continued for six years.

Finally, the Palestinians rebelled. As we complete this book, Intifadet El Aqsa has been raging for more than a year and five months. Need we add that this new intifada is challenging Israel's hegemony and its oppressive military rule?

Let us be more explicit. When the first intifada was terminated, a large percentage of Palestinians trusted the Israelis that their life would change for the better. This trust was expressed in some of the narratives of the freedom fighters that we presented in previous chapters. Since 1993, the Palestinian spokespersons and lay people have repeatedly pointed out that their trust was betrayed, often by cruel deeds and by harsh decrees of the Israeli military. In many respects, during the years of the so-called peace process, Palestinian life in the Gaza Strip became more sordid, less free. Some of the details of Israel's continual harsh military rule of the Gaza Strip in the years following the signing of the 1993 peace accords are described in the two newsletters that appear in the appendix of this book.

Many Palestinians state that the most significant item among the many items in the Oslo Agreement that Israel did not fulfill was its refusal to evacuate all the Palestinian territory which was to be evacuated according to that agreement. The territory to be evacuated included all the West Bank and the Gaza Strip except the Israeli settlements and Jerusalem. The Oslo Agreement stated that this total evacuation was to be completed by May 1999. It was not completed by that date, which was more than fifteen months before the second Palestinian rebellion commenced. Nor was there any movement toward evacuating that Palestinian land when Intifadet El Aqsa erupted.

Furthermore, during the entire period since the signing of the Oslo Agreement in 1993, reporters citing World Bank research announced that Israel continued its economic exploitation and political oppression of the Palestinian people. This exploitation and oppression continued even under the leadership of the ministers of the Labor Party, such as Ehud Barak, who announced that they were pro-peace. As noted in Chapter 1 and as described in detail in the appendix, this oppression included, among other things, denying the majority of Palestinians freedom of movement and forcefully creating conditions that condemned the large majority of Palestinians to live in abject poverty. It also included enlarging the territory of the Jewish settlements in the Gaza Strip and on the West Bank, which were initially settled on land illegally confiscated from Palestinians. The continual enlargement of the settlements led to confiscation of more and more Palestinian land for these settlements.

Based on our own experience as workers for human rights and on facts presented in a host of nonbiased publications, we can state categorically that from 1993 until today, during the so-called peace process, Israel has continued to act as a brutal occupying and colonial power in the Gaza Strip and on the West Bank. Israel consistently and forcefully rejected all attempts by the Palestinian people to live in freedom. After seven years, the Palestinian people recognized that the Oslo Peace Accord had not brought freedom or economic development. The peace accord led to greater burdens on their daily lives, burdens which included economic hardships and daily military harassment. In addition, the Palestinians continued to describe many incidents in which the Israelis continued to trample upon their dignity.

The conclusions are evident. They disclose the genuine meaning of the second Palestinian rebellion. Like the first intifada, Intifadet El Aqsa is a struggle for freedom; it is the Palestinian people's fight for an independent state of their own. Palestinian spokespersons are stating the truth when they announce: The current Palestinian rebellion is a forceful rejection of Israel's ruthless military occupation of Palestinian land and its brutal oppression of the freedom of the Palestinians.

Since the eruption of Intifadet El Aqsa, the situation in this area of the world has become much more complicated. At first glance, you will note that the overall struggle for peace and justice in the Gaza Strip and the Near East has been undermined. The major recent reason for this undermining of the quest for a just peace, we believe, is Israel's ruthless military response to Intifadet El Aqsa.

It is now the moment to call a spade a spade. Israel's harsh response to Intifadet El Aqsa has included many war crimes. (We shall present the accepted definition of a war crime in a moment.) These war crimes were initiated and performed under the command of Major General Shaul Mufaz, Israel's chief of staff and the commander of its armed forces. Unfortunately, the crimes were supported by the Israeli governments, including the Labor government of Ehud Barak. Even today, under the government of Ariel Sharon, Israeli armed forces under the command of Major General Mufaz continue to commit war crimes.

The purposeful commission of war crimes is today broadly condemned. Hence, our statement that Major General Shaul Mufaz is responsible for war crimes against the Palestinian people needs to be supported by evidence. In what follows, we shall provide this evidence. We shall look carefully, albeit briefly, at some of the more brutal war crimes that Israeli forces have performed since the eruption of Intifadet El Aqsa on September 28, 2000, against the Palestinians who are struggling for freedom. This concentration on the war crimes committed by Israelis should add to the understanding of the Palestinian struggle for freedom described by the narrators in the previous section—a struggle that Israeli forces are attempting to strangle.

First, however, let us recall that in 1998 in Rome, the charter establishing the International Criminal Court under the United Nations was negotiated and agreed upon, and the principles that would guide its activities were proclaimed. Since then, the charter has been signed by more than 140 nations, including Israel. At last count, the charter has been ratified by 66 nations. According to the Rome charter, the International Criminal Court would have authority to hold individuals (rather than states) accountable for failing to obey international humanitarian law. Thus the court could hold accountable those individuals who gave the orders that led to, or who personally participated in, crimes such as genocide, crimes against humanity, and war crimes.

In the Israeli press it was explained that in the charter establishing the International Criminal Court, a war crime is defined as "a purposeful attack, done with the knowledge that the attack can lead to the death or wounding of uninvolved citizens, or to the destruction of property that belongs to uninvolved citizens, or to the ruining of the natural environment."

In this book, we accept this definition of a war crime. In what follows, we shall briefly show that the Israeli Defense Force, commanded by Major General Shaul Mufaz, have purposely committed all three kinds of war crimes described in the above definition.

Let us start with the killing of Palestinian children who are under the age of fourteen. To date, a year and five months after Intifadet El Aqsa erupted, more than 600 Palestinians, most of them civilians, have been killed by the Israeli armed forces. Quite a few were killed in the struggles and demonstrations of the Palestinians against Israeli oppression. There is still disagreement among human rights organizations as to the exact number of the children who were killed by Israeli bullets and shells. What is generally agreed is that the Israeli armed forces killed at least sixty Palestinian children under the age of fourteen, most of them much younger than fourteen. Quite a few were killed in Israeli-initiated military operations, such as rocket attacks by Apache helicopters. Some of the Palestinian children were shot dead by Israeli snipers when they demonstrated against the Israeli occupation. These demonstrations occurred on Palestinian land, not even on land that the Israelis had confiscated. A few Palestinian children were shot and killed when they threw rocks at an Israeli army pillbox.

Rivca Gordon and Haim Gordon have seen these Israeli pillboxes close up. They have spoken to the Israeli soldiers serving in them and have taken pictures of the pillboxes. On the basis of this testimony, we can state categorically that the rocks thrown by Palestinian youths from outside the pillbox could never have endangered the Israeli soldiers who were in the pillbox.

According to Palestinian sources, most of the demonstrating children who were shot dead by Israeli soldiers were 200 meters or more from an Israeli army post. Since they had no firearms, they definitely did not endanger the Israeli soldiers. Of course, they never endangered the snipers. However, many Palestinian children were killed without ever participating in any rejection of the Israeli occupation. They were merely in a civilian area that the Israeli forces decided to shell or to bomb and were killed there.

Iman Haju was three and a half months old when suddenly, in the middle of a day in early May 2001, her grandparents' home in the city of Khan Yunis in the Gaza Strip was hit by two Israeli tank shells. Iman was killed instantly; her cousins, mother, and grandmother were wounded. Israel apologized. But Israel did not admit that it was a war crime to order its tanks to shell Palestinian buildings that housed unarmed civilians. Iman was not the only civilian killed by Israel's continual shelling of Palestinian houses in the Gaza Strip. Nor was Iman Haju the only child killed by such attacks. During the first year of Intifadet El Aqsa, every few days Palestinian houses were shelled by Israeli tanks or by Apache helicopters. Again, the exact numbers are not available, but it is evident that more than 15,000 unarmed, uninvolved Palestinian civilians have been wounded in the continual shooting at civilians and shelling of civilian homes. According to Palestinian sources, around 20 percent of these wounded will be permanently handicapped.

Major General Shaul Mufaz has never issued an army order notifying the Israeli soldiers under his command that they should not shoot Palestinian civilians, especially children.

On a visit to the Gaza Strip on March 25, 2001, in which Israeli Knesset members were accompanied by Rivca Gordon and Haim Gordon, the group heard the following report from A'id El Abadla, the mayor of the township of El Garara. A'id El Abadla explained that his township included relatively large sections of agricultural land. Through that land there was a four-kilometer road along which some of the Israeli settlers who resided in the Gaza Strip traveled to their settlements. Since the eruption of Intifadet El Aqsa, the settlers were not safe when traveling on that road; although they traveled in convoys, guarded by Israeli army vehicles, they had been shot at by Palestinians. The Israeli response to the shooting was to raze all Palestinian land on both sides of the road, which would supposedly ensure the safe passage each day of several dozen settlers. Remember, all these settlers are living on land that was confiscated by Israel from the Palestinians.

What exactly happened in El Garara when Israel decided to raze the land on both sides of the road? A'id El Abadla told us that during one of the recent nights, a large unit which included many Israeli army bulldozers and soldiers came, uprooted, demolished, and destroyed everything that existed within a range of up to 300 meters from both sides of the road that the Israeli settlers used to drive to their settlements.

Here is the list that A'id El Abadla gave us of the property that Israeli forces destroyed in one night. Thirty-four houses were reduced to rubble; in many of them furniture and personal goods were destroyed and domestic fowls and livestock were buried alive. Fifty-five houses were partially demolished. The Israeli forces uprooted, destroyed, or stole the following numbers of trees that were in the 300-meter range of the road: 3,315 olive trees, 1,189 palm trees,

5,017 orange trees, 3,389 almond trees, 135 fig trees, and 4,489 other trees. The Israeli army bulldozers also destroyed three wells, breaking and fragmenting their pumps and wrecking their motors. In addition, the bulldozers pulverized fifteen sheep pens and razed to the ground a plant nursery.

Even if Israel announced that some of the Palestinians living along the road helped the snipers who were shooting at Israeli cars in the convoys of settlers, no evidence was given that even some of the destroyed property belonged to these Palestinians. Perhaps the property of those who helped the snipers begins 500 meters from the road. And why did Israel destroy wells and their pumps? We can safely state that at least 90 percent of the property destroyed by Israeli bulldozers and army forces belonged to uninvolved Palestinians. In addition, recall again the centuries-old principle: A person is innocent until proved guilty. Hence, destroying the Palestinian property in El Garara without examining whether the owner of the property had any relationship to Palestinian snipers was a war crime.

El Garara is just one township. Yet it is a township which is in an area that Israeli military sources term a "friction area" between Israelis and Palestinians. Multiply the destruction in El Garara by, say, a factor of thirty, and one begins to comprehend the devastation that Israeli forces have wreaked on Palestinian property in the Occupied Territories since September 28, 2000. We want to list some numbers provided to us by the Palestinian Finance Ministry concerning the destruction of Palestinian civilian property by Israeli forces. These numbers describe the destruction of Palestinian property up until April 15, 2001. Since then, under the command of Major General Shaul Mufaz, the destruction of Palestinian property belonging to civilians has continued unabated.

According to the Palestinian Finance Ministry, during this time in the Palestinian territories occupied by Israel, Israeli armed forces destroyed 4,080 houses of civilian Palestinians, and uprooted and demolished 170,000 trees belonging to Palestinians—these included olive, citrus, and palm trees that take decades to reach maturity. Israeli forces also reduced to rubble several dozen Palestinian greenhouses, destroyed Palestinian irrigation networks, and killed livestock. All of this was done, supposedly, in order to ensure the lives and well-being of the settlers who are living on land in the Occupied Territories, land that was confiscated from Palestinians.

These facts indicate that, in relation to Palestinian property, Major General Shaul Mufaz already has quite a few war crimes to his name. We can state that his deeds illustrate the saying that describes the Roman occupation of Britain, cited by Tacitus in *The Agricola*: "They create a desolation and call it peace."[1]

It is evident that Israel's uprooting of 170,000 Palestinian trees during a period of less than seven months, for so-called security reasons, is a destruction of the environment. Such is especially true in the Mediterranean climate of Palestine, which borders on the desert. But the uprooted trees are only one of many examples of destruction of the environment that Israeli soldiers under the command of Major General Shaul Mufaz have conducted. We shall only mention three other examples.

Israeli army bulldozers have dug deep ditches through Palestinian agricultural land, ruining crops and destroying the natural environment. The ditches were dug as part of the closures that Israeli forces have forced upon Palestinian towns and cities. The ditches helped the Israeli forces to limit the freedom of movement of the residents of the Palestinian villages, towns, and cities.

These same bulldozers have also constructed high dirt ramparts on many Palestinian roads, which do not allow cars to pass on the road. Again, the ramparts were constructed in order to close Palestinians in their cities, towns, and villages. These closures have forced many Palestinians to find new dirt roads in order to leave their villages and towns, again ruining the environment. The Israeli bulldozers have also destroyed natural irrigation channels. In addition, Israel continues to pave special roads on Palestinian land in order to make it easier to enforce the occupation of that Palestinian land. Each new paved road contributes to the destruction of the environment. Most such instances of ruining the environment occurred in the West Bank, but the Gaza Strip also suffered from all three examples.

Israel's war crimes have not been ignored by some of the citizens and politicians in Israel. Here are three examples. In response to one of the Israeli army's more vicious attacks on civilian Palestinians, Knesset member Eisam Makhul, in a speech in the Knesset, called Major General Shaul Mufaz a war criminal. On April 20, 2001, Israel's current minister of transportation, Ephrayim Sneh, was quoted in the Israeli daily newspaper *Yediot Ahronot*, saying that he was against Prime Minister Sharon's harsh policies. Sneh added that he wanted everyone to know that "Sharon will appear at the International Criminal Court at The Hague—without me." In the summer of 2001, the former Knesset member and journalist Uri Avneri wrote in the Israeli daily newspaper *Maariv* and in the *International Herald Tribune* an editorial opinion in which he condemned Israel's brutal abuse of the human rights of the Palestinians. In that essay Avneri listed and condemned some of the war crimes of Major General Shaul Mufaz.

But these responses have not altered the actions of the Israeli army in the Gaza Strip and on the West Bank. Today, in the winter of 2002, the residents of the Gaza Strip are living in deep misery—a misery that is forced upon them by the Israeli army and by Israel's political decisions. The residents of the Gaza Strip are also exposed to war crimes committed by the Israeli army.

Look at it closely. The Gaza Strip resembles a large, fenced-in concentration camp. In this camp, Israeli tanks, guard towers, and pillboxes manned by many soldiers stand at major junctions and in other so-called "military sensitive areas." We are speaking of dozens of Israeli tanks, dozens of guard towers, and many pillboxes. The Israeli soldiers manning these tanks and towers can open fire on Palestinians whenever they see fit to do so. Consequently, the Palestinians living in this fenced-in area, in this Israeli-created ghetto, are subjected to arbitrary Israeli military actions which include shooting of civilians, razing of property, politically initiated poverty, the ruining of health, and the destruction of the environment. In addition, by creating blockades, Israeli forces at times create days of hunger in certain towns and cities.

No wonder that many residents of the Gaza Strip announce that they have lost hope in the possibility of reaching a peaceful and just agreement with Israel. These Palestinians see the Israeli military trampling upon their freedom and dignity every day, with no end in sight.

This terrible situation leads to a major question to be considered by the readers of this book. What do the preceding narratives of freedom fighters disclose about the current situation and the future of the Gaza Strip? Do these narratives suggest that there is hope? We respond, albeit partially, to these questions in our concluding chapter.

NOTE

1. Tacitus, *The Agricola and The Germania.* Trans. H. Mattingly and S.A. Handford (London: Penguin Books, 1970), 81.

Chapter 10

A Just Peace

The philosopher Martin Heidegger repeatedly pointed out that beginnings are rare moments. They are cut off from the past and point to the future, to what is beyond. In order to relate to a beginning, therefore, you must not look at it through the eyes of someone contemplating the past. Rather, you must try to grasp the spirit of the unique moment which was cut off from all the moments that preceded it and look only toward the future. With Heidegger's insight in mind, we authors believe that the humble beginning of this book might have occurred on a wintry day in December 1990, in the Gaza Strip.

On that day, five Israeli Knesset members accompanied Rivca Gordon and Haim Gordon on a visit to the Gaza Strip; the goal of the visit was to learn about some of the manifestations of Israeli oppression of the Palestinians during the intifada. At the request of Rivca and Haim, Taher Shriteh hired a small local minibus and driver; Taher served as the so-called tour guide of the group of visitors. The tour was quite successful; the Knesset members later told the media that they had been appalled by the poverty and misery of the Palestinians, especially by the misery in the refugee camps. However, there was one encounter during the tour—at Jebalia Refugee Camp—that the Knesset members did not mention. We wish to briefly recall that encounter, which we consider to be a humble beginning that looks to the future. As such, the encounter also conveys a central message of this book.

For some reason that we don't remember, on that day Jebalia Refugee Camp had already been under Israeli army curfew for more than a week. How does Jebalia Refugee Camp look when it is under an Israeli army curfew? In one word: desolate. No one was allowed to enter or to leave the camp. Palestinians without special permits, that is, 98 percent of the population, were not allowed out of the huts and shacks that served them as homes. Israeli armed vehicles and groups of soldiers patrolled the roads and alleys of the camp, endeavoring to strictly enforce the curfew.

Taher knew of the curfew. He did not tell us. He chose to enter Jebalia Refugee Camp through one of the bumpy, untraveled roads where the Israeli army usually did not set up a checkpoint. Only after we were well inside the refugee camp did we begin to suspect that there was a curfew; but the minibus had already stopped at one of the concrete huts that UNRWA had set up more than three decades ago to house Palestinians.

The Palestinian woman who lived with her family in the bleak hut was reticent. Her husband was not present, and her children were at a neighbor's shack. She explained in Arabic that since the intifada she and her family were eating only pita bread and oil that arrived from UNRWA, together with some tomatoes they received free at the market. Indeed the small space in the hut that served as a kitchen was bare of any foods. An Arab Knesset member translated her halting sentences into Hebrew.

Before we left, the woman also mentioned the curfew. Suddenly, the Knesset members grasped their situation. They told us that if there was a curfew, they preferred to cut short their visit in Jebalia Refugee Camp. They did not want to anger the Israeli army.

But when we left the hut, there was a crowd of a few dozen Palestinians from the neighborhood standing around the minibus. They stood there quietly, waiting for the Israeli Knesset members. While we were inside the UNRWA shack, Taher had knocked on a few doors and invited the residents to meet the Israeli Knesset members. The word had spread and they were there, Palestinians from Jebalia Refugee Camp defying the curfew in order to meet the Israeli legislators. Many of the Palestinians spoke Hebrew, and soon each Knesset member was speaking with a group of Palestinians, discussing the possibilities of peace, of justice, of freedom for the Palestinians.

We don't remember the exact details of the discussions, but the fact that they occurred is most significant. They showed us that even in harsh circumstances of intifada and curfew, many Palestinians in the impoverished refugee camps, and also many Israelis, seek and will continue to seek a just, peaceful solution to the ongoing conflict.

The meeting in Jebalia Refugee Camp can be viewed as the humble beginning of this book because, like many Palestinians and Israelis, we authors are actively seeking justice and peace for the residents of this area of the world. The meeting shows, as this book shows, that trust and dialogue are central to such seeking. The possibility of human beings developing trust and engaging in dialogue with each other is always a source of hope.

Before looking at other possibilities for hope in the future, we should briefly summarize what the narratives in this book teach about the recent past of the Gaza Strip. The most important point concerning this past is simple and clear.

The Palestinian freedom fighters from the Gaza Strip, whose narratives we present in this book, belong to a people that have been oppressed and exploited for more than half a century. Egypt was the military ruler of the Gaza Strip from 1948 until 1967. Israel has been the military ruler and oppressor since 1967. The narrators hated this military rule and oppression. They were hurt by it and found ways to rebel.

In comprehending the lives and actions of these six persons who fought against the Israeli military occupation, we must always remember that the Gaza Strip, with its hundreds of thousands of refugees, with its third and fourth generation of Palestinians living in refugee camps, is an area where misery is widespread. We must also remember that for the past thirty-five years, that misery is largely the direct result of Israeli political decisions and Israel's military occupation of the Gaza Strip. During these three and a half decades, for the large majority of Palestinians, living in the Gaza Strip meant being condemned to straitened circumstances. For the children of these Palestinians, growing up in the Gaza Strip meant being condemned to poverty, misery, and the daily denial of one's dignity, human rights, and basic freedoms. Is it strange that some of the narrators express a profound rage and others embrace extreme views?

Indeed, for people who adhere to liberal values, some of the views of the Palestinian narrators may seem quite extreme or fanatic. We authors agree that, usually, excessive political positions and extreme fanatic stances do not lead to peace and justice. Yet, we also want to stress that extremists will often find fertile ground among people who are condemned to live in poverty and misery, and who daily suffer from injustice for spreading their tenets and beliefs.

Hence we can state a major conclusion that emerges from all the narratives. The first step toward justice for the Palestinians residing in the Gaza Strip must be the immediate termination of the Israeli military occupation of Palestinian land.

Given this situation, what are additional sources of hope for a better future that perhaps emerge from the narratives? Where can the Palestinian people find those refreshing springs of human vitality that encourage hope? Given the volatile political situation of the Middle East, we can only proffer some partial answers.

Whether they say so or not, the narrators cited in the previous chapters recognize an important political principle. They recognize that despite their representing some of the different political and religious groups and views that are currently dominant in the Gaza Strip, the fight for freedom means working together while acknowledging their differences. This recognition is wise. It accepts the fact that tolerance, respect of the freedom of the Other, and accepting the fact that the Other may differ in relating to the current situation is central to living a life of political freedom. Hence, respecting the freedom of other persons and other groups in one's society is a source of strength.

Put differently, this recognition and acceptance of differing views is a source of hope. It embodies and inspires the hope that the Palestinians in the Gaza Strip—united in their struggle for freedom despite their differences—will find the courage and the strength to continue their struggle for freedom and dignity, even after Israel terminates its ruthless military rule of the area.

Yet the greatest source of hope is the freedom fighters themselves. The narratives disclose that these people and many of their contemporaries are determined to struggle for the freedom of the Palestinian people. Their lives and struggles add moments of untarnished glory to the Palestinian quest for freedom.

Appendixes

What follows are two issues of the newsletter *Struggle*, written by Haim Gordon and Rivca Gordon. *Struggle* is published twice a year by the Foundation for Democratic Education in Israel. Both newsletters deal with the cruel and oppressive military rule of Israel in the Gaza Strip after the end of the Palestinian intifada in 1993, and with the beginning of the so-called peace process.

The first newsletter is dated October 1997 and discusses the oppression of basic freedoms of the Palestinians residing in the Gaza Strip. The second newsletter is dated October 2000 and discusses the plight of the fishermen in the Gaza Strip. Taken together, the newsletters present some of the details of the continual Israeli oppression of the Palestinians during the so-called peace process. They also add substance to the many facts presented in the book concerning the difficulties of daily life in the Gaza Strip under Israeli military rule.

Gaza, 1997:
Israeli Oppression of Basic Freedoms

Haim Gordon and Rivca Gordon

INTRODUCTION

Has the signing of the 1993 peace accords between Israel and the PLO brought greater freedom to the residents of the Gaza Strip? The answer to this question is a resounding "no." Who is responsible for this situation? The answer is in the details that we present in this newsletter. But as the title of this newsletter indicates, Israel's oppression of basic freedoms of the Palestinians is the major reason for the sad developments in the Gaza Strip. In what follows we describe some of the major features of that ongoing oppression, which has become much more destructive of human rights under the Netanyahu government.

GEOGRAPHY

The Gaza Strip is approximately 46 kilometers long. It is 12.5 kilometers wide at its southern end and 8 kilometers wide at its northern end. To the north and east the Gaza Strip borders Israel. To the south it borders Egypt. To the west is the Mediterranean Sea. The Strip is surrounded by a high fence which day and night is patrolled and guarded by Israeli troops on the northern and eastern borders, and by Egyptian soldiers on the southern border. The Mediterranean Sea is patrolled by Israeli gunboats. There are only five official entrances to the Strip. Erez checkpoint is for all tourists and Israelis, except settlers, who wish to enter the Gaza Strip, and for all Palestinians who wish to enter Israel. Some goods are also transferred from the Gaza Strip to Israel through Erez checkpoint. Nachal Oz checkpoint and Gush Katif checkpoint are for Israeli settlers who wish to drive to their settlements. Karni passage is solely for transferring goods to and from the Strip. Rafah checkpoint is for Israelis and

Palestinians who wish to travel to and from Egypt. Egyptians and tourists traveling from Egypt to Israel by land can also use this checkpoint. The Israel Defense Force decides who among Israelis and Palestinians is permitted to use these entrances and when that person can use the entrances.

Although there has been no recent census, it is acknowledged that at least one million people live in the Gaza Strip; 70 percent of the inhabitants are refugees from the 1948 War with Israel or descendents of those refugees. According to U.N. estimates, it is the most densely populated area on earth. It is also acknowledged that at least 50 percent of the refugees, around 465,000 people, still reside in refugee camps. At most there are 6,000 Jewish settlers who reside in the Gaza Strip. As a result of Israel's confiscations of Palestinian land during its twenty-eight years of occupation, 50 percent of the land suited for agriculture in the Strip is currently under Israeli domination; much of this land is leased to the settlers by the Israeli government. Thus 6,000 Israeli settlers have choice land, while hundreds of thousands of Palestinians suffer in refugee camps without work or property.

According to the Oslo Agreement, Israeli gunboats may prevent Gaza fishing boats from sailing further than twelve kilometers from the shore. In practice, however, the 800 Palestinian fishing boats that fish along the Strip, which employ 4,000 fishermen, do not sail more than four or five kilometers from the shore, since they have been repeatedly shot at by Israeli gunboats when they have ventured further. Palestinian complaints concerning these fishermen have fallen on deaf ears.

FREEDOM OF MOVEMENT

Although there are no exact figures, it is safe to say that no more than 10 percent of the residents of the Gaza Strip can leave it. (We believe that the true number is closer to 5 percent.) Ninety percent, 900,000 Palestinians, are condemned to live in this ghetto—many Palestinians call it a cage—with no possibility of traveling to another area of the world, including the West Bank or neighboring countries such as Israel, Jordan, or Egypt. The two reasons for this situation are direct results of Israeli policy. The first is the widespread poverty in Gaza. The second is the decision to prevent people from leaving Gaza for what is termed "security reasons."

In 1987 the per capita income in the Gaza Strip was around $1,500. In 1997 the per capita income is around $750. Since the signing of the peace accords in 1993, the per capita income has continually declined. This increasing poverty is very much a result of Israel's political and economic policies, which today include closures and the limitation of a free flow of good and services. During the twenty-eight years of its domination, Israel did not allow the development of industries in the Gaza Strip and did not invest at all in Palestinian infrastructure. It is well-nigh inconceivable that an entrepreneur would wish to establish a new industry or factory in the Gaza Strip when there is no free flow of goods and services and without a reliable infrastructure, such as a regular flow of electricity. Hence, it is no surprise that no major industries have been established and no factories have been built in the Gaza Strip since 1993.

Limitation of the number of Palestinian workers who can come to Israel is another reason for the poverty. In 1987, before the Gulf War, which led to the expulsion of tens of thousands of Palestinians who worked in the Gulf States and Iraq and the return of many of them to the West Bank and the Gaza Strip, more than 100,000 workers from the Gaza Strip came legally to work in Israel every day. At least 30,000 came illegally. Today, due to closures and the so-called security reasons, at most 21,000 laborers from the Gaza Strip work in Israel daily—when there is no closure. The other 100,000 who used to work in Israel, together with those workers who returned from the Gulf States, are unemployed.

For many tens of thousands of people living in the Gaza Strip, the disposable funds are much lower than $750 per year. Since there is a wealthy elite in the Gaza Strip, and the per capita income is an average sum, there are tens of thousands of Palestinians whose disposable funds are much less than $750 per year. According to committees of the Palestinian Legislative Council, there is widespread corruption in the administrative branches of the Palestinian Authority. The result is that hundreds of thousands of Palestinians do not have the funds necessary for leaving Gaza, even if they could receive permission to travel beyond the ghetto in which they live. These Palestinians are denied one of the most basic of freedoms—the freedom of movement. This denial of freedom of movement is one result of Israel's policy of continual economic strangulation of the Gaza Strip, a policy which has been implemented daily for three decades.

To some of the Gazans who have funds, freedom of movement is denied for so-called security reasons. However, quite often this denial has nothing to do with security. It is merely evil oppression. For instance, for weeks after the second suicide bombing in the summer of 1997, on September 4, members of the Palestinian Legislative Council residing in Gaza, including the head of the opposition, Dr. Haidar Abdul Shafi, were not permitted to go to Ramalah in the West Bank for meetings of the council. Israel knows that Dr. Haidar Abdul Shafi, who headed the Palestinian delegation to the peace talks in Washington, is not a security risk. Yet for weeks he was not allowed to leave the Gaza Strip for what were called security reasons.

Another example is Taher Shriteh, who is thirty-seven years old and works as a reporter in Gaza for Reuters News Agency, CBS, and the *New York Times*. During the intifada he was jailed ten times by the Israelis, without being charged; his longest period of incarceration was thirty-eight days during the Gulf War. He has also been jailed twice by the Palestinian Authority for publishing reports that it disliked; again, he was never charged. On March 16, 1993, the United States National Press Club in Washington, D.C. awarded the International Freedom of Press Award to Taher Shriteh. Four months earlier Taher had been jailed and put on one of the buses of the 400 Palestinians being deported to Lebanon by Israel. Due to internal and international pressure he was taken off the bus and returned to Gaza before the buses crossed the border.

Since receiving the International Freedom of Press Award in Washington, Taher has not been allowed to enter Israel or even to leave Gaza in order to go to Egypt. In December 1995, through the help of Arafat's office, he was allowed to visit Spain for a conference of reporters; he traveled through Egypt. As this newsletter was going to press, Israeli security officers decided to not allow Taher to attend a seminar of the International Visitor's Program sponsored by the United States Information Agency, held in Washington, D.C. He received a formal invitation to attend this seminar from Martin Indyk, the United States ambassador to Israel. Only after we intervened and enlisted the help of Knesset member Yossi Sarid was Taher allowed to travel to the United States through Egypt. Taher Shriteh is not a security risk to Israel; he is not a suicide bomber. Thus, the decision not to allow him to enter Israel or go to the United States to attend a seminar is merely an evil Israeli decision to punish him for his good reporting.

THE SAFE PASSAGE

There is also no freedom of movement between the two areas ruled by the Palestinian Authority: the Gaza Strip and the West Bank. In the agreement signed on September 28, 1995, between Yitzchak Rabin and Yasser Arafat, it is clearly stated: "There shall be a safe passage connecting the West Bank with the Gaza Strip for movement of persons, vehicles and goods … Israel will ensure safe passage for persons and transportation during daylight hours (from sunrise to sunset), … but in any event not less than 10 hours a day." More than two years after its signing, nothing relating to the safe passage has been implemented by Israel.

One result of not implementing the safe passage is that moving goods from the West Bank to Gaza or from Gaza to the West Bank has become very difficult and expensive. We will not explain in detail the Kafkaesque regulations that Israel has imposed on the Gazans who wish to transfer goods to the West Bank or buy goods produced there. For some of the small firms in Gaza that relied on the market of the West Bank, these regulations have made the transfer of goods so expensive and difficult that they gave up and either closed down or drastically reduced their production. Such a result adds to the poverty in the Gaza Strip, which in turn curtails freedom of movement of Palestinians.

Even Gazans with financial means are forced to suffer from Israel's decision to not fulfill its obligation of providing a safe passage between Gaza and the West Bank. Relatively wealthy merchants in Gaza who have investments in the West Bank are usually not given permission to enter Israel so as to travel to the West Bank. At least 120 of these merchants have had to travel to Egypt, from there fly to Amman in Jordan, and from there cross the Jordan River to the West Bank in order to deal with their investments on the spot. After they have completed their work, these merchants have had to travel back to Gaza in the same roundabout manner, thus wasting at least two days and great expense on a trip that requires, at most, three to four hours from Gaza to reach any destination in the West Bank.

In addition, at least 1,200 students from Gaza who began their studies in universities in the West Bank have not been given permission to return to the West Bank to complete their studies for so-called security reasons. The security reasons have nothing to do with the individual students. The large majority of these students are not suspected of terrorism. Their being denied permission to travel through Israel has to do with the fact that most suicide bombers in Israel in the past years were under the age of thirty; hence, Israel does not allow people under thirty to travel from Gaza to the West Bank. The establishment of a safe passage would have allowed the students to reach their universities.

CLOSURES

The policy of closures is one of the most wicked manifestations of Israel's attempts to coerce the Palestinians. It was initiated during the Gulf War in 1991 and even then made the Gaza Strip into a cage, as the residents refer to it. Since the signing of the peace accords, the policy of closures has continued, especially after a terrorist or suicide attack against Israeli population, when the terrorists are traced to the Occupied Territories or the Gaza Strip. Also, during Israeli holidays the Gazans are subject to closure and not permitted to leave the Strip. From May 1994 until the end of 1996, there were 300 days of closure of the Gaza Strip. During a closure no Gazans are allowed to work in Israel, and even travel of seriously ill people to Israeli hospitals is severely restricted. The flow of goods to and from Israel and abroad is stopped and then very slowly resumed. It has been repeatedly stated that the policy of closures is a manner of collective punishment and has little to do with stopping terrorist attacks.

On July 30, 1997, under Binyamin Netanyahu's evil government, the policy of closures attained a new level of cynicism. Immediately after two suicide bombers exploded themselves in the Machaneh Yehuda market, Netanyahu ordered an absolute closure of all Occupied Territories, including the Gaza Strip. From the beginning there was little evidence that the bombers came from the areas under the Palestinian Authority, such as the Gaza Strip. Indeed, the latest report, based on circumstantial evidence, states that the suicide bombers came from a small town near Nablus under Israeli rule, where Israel has sole responsibility for security. Israeli authorities have not published any conclusive proof linking these bombers to any Palestinian organization active in suicide bombing in the past. Nor have they published proof that these suicide bombers received help from Palestinians under Palestinian rule. The closest Israel came to such proof was the statement that experts found the explosives to be similar to those found by Palestinian police in an explosives laboratory in Beit Lehem, supposedly set up by the Hamas. But the so-called similarity of explosives, which experts from the Palestinian Authority deny, is hardly evidence that the suicide bombers were linked to the Hamas. Anyone with a handbook on explosives can make similar bombs.

Whatever the final outcome of the investigation, no one in Israel has stated that the suicide bombers came from the Gaza Strip or had links to the Gaza Strip. Nonetheless, Netanyahu decided that Arafat is to blame, and in addition to the closure on the West Bank, he closed the Gaza Strip and froze Palestinian money in Israeli banks. International organizations and some governments declared this freezing of funds to be robbery, but even as this newsletter goes to press Netanyahu has refused to release all the money. More importantly, Netanyahu demanded that Arafat arrest and lock up anyone who is affiliated with the Hamas in the Gaza Strip, even if the person has no link to the bombing. He wanted Arafat to act like the police officer in the movie *Casablanca*. This officer sees Humphrey Bogart shoot the Nazi colonel and instructs his men to round up "the usual suspects." Arafat responded that he does not lock up people for their views and that to lock up Hamas leaders or other Palestinian religious dignitaries in the Gaza Strip, he needs evidence linking them to the suicide bombers. Netanyahu had no facts or evidence to present; at least no such evidence was published in the Israeli media.

In past years the Israeli government, including the Netanyahu government, has always presented the identities of the suicide bombers in great detail: their full names, the towns where they lived, the names of their immediate and extended family, where they received training, who helped them, and much additional anecdotal information. Since it is very difficult to believe that Netanyahu would refrain from presenting evidence linking the Machaneh Yehuda suicide bombers to the Palestinian Authority if he had it—evidence that could embarrass Arafat and the Palestinian Authority—it is clear that until now he was deceiving the public when he said that he had hard evidence but did not present it. But the international press and especially the United States administration accepted Netanyahu's deceit, and accused Arafat and the Palestinians in the Occupied Territories of terrorism. Both the mainstream international media and the United States administration refused to accept the fact that there is no evidence that the suicide bombers originated in the Gaza Strip or had any links to the Gaza Strip. Hence, they refused to condemn the closure imposed on the Gaza Strip and other draconian measures that Netanyahu implemented, which bring suffering upon hundreds of thousands of innocent Palestinians.

The responses of the Netanyahu government were repeated with greater wrath after a second suicide bombing on September 4, 1997, again in Jerusalem, on Ben Yehuda Street. No evidence linked the three suicide bombers to the Gaza Strip. But Netanyahu immediately imposed a lengthy closure on the Gaza Strip together with a closure on the West Bank. To blunt criticism, the government obtained a court order which does not allow the media to report on the in-vestigation of the bombing, including where the suicide bombers originated. When the Palestinian Authority again notified the press that these bombers did not originate in an area under their rule, they were again ignored by the inter-national press and by the United States administration, both of which again ac-cepted Netanyahu's demagoguery. Again, published Israeli reports which link the suicide bombers to Palestinians indicate that they came from the same town near Nablus, which is under Israeli rule and responsibility for security. There is no published fact that can condemn any person in the Gaza Strip for links to these bombers, yet the closure on the Gaza Strip was imposed and brought great suffering.

SUMMARY

The Gaza Strip today is a large ghetto populated by one million people, most of whom are burdened by poverty and denied freedom of movement. The pol-icies responsible for this poverty and lack of freedom originated in Jerusalem in the decisions made by the governments of Israel, including the government of Labor and Meretz. The closures imposed on the Gaza Strip are unjust and based on deception of the public. They are a denial of basic human rights. Indeed, the closures are an unjust collective punishment, very often for deeds no Gazan did, imposed on a million Palestinians. Furthermore, the closures have not halted the terrorist attacks to which they are a supposed response.

Finally, we wish to add what should be evident: By unjustly, forcefully op-pressing the freedom of the people in the Gaza Strip, who are our next-door neighbors, the Israeli government is also ruining the democratic principles upon which it rests.

Appendix B

Fishermen in Gaza

Haim Gordon and Rivca Gordon

INTRODUCTION

Three years ago, in Newsletter No. 16 published in October 1997, we opened the introduction with the question: "Has the signing of the 1993 peace accords between Israel and the PLO brought greater freedom to the residents of the Gaza Strip?" Our answer was a resounding "no." Three years later, our answer to the above question has not changed. Freedom in the Gaza Strip, which the residents call their large cage, is still very restricted and limited daily by Israeli policies and military power. As one former freedom fighter from Gaza, Tawfik Abu Khoosa, told us, "There are still more than 700,000 residents of the Gaza Strip, out of the 1.1 million people who live here, who do not even know what the entrance to the Gaza Strip at Erez checkpoint looks like—since there is no reason for them to approach that entrance. They know that they will never pass through it or see it from the Israeli side. They are stuck here in the Gaza Strip, behind the well-patrolled barbed wire fences that surround us, inside the big jail that you Israelis created."

In this newsletter, however, we do not want to explain, once again, the harsh reality confronting all of the residents of the Gaza Strip. Nor do we want to explain how this harsh reality is a result of unjustified Israeli policies. Instead, we want to focus on one small group of Palestinians who reside in the Gaza Strip and who, as they pursue their daily struggle to make a living, have suffered from continual Israeli harassment and repeated unjustified violence by Israeli forces. This continual harassment and unjustified Israeli violence has not at all changed since the signing of the peace accords. It continues to this day. This small group of hard-working people, who suffer Israeli harassment and violence, is made up of the 3,353 fisherman in the Gaza Strip. We believe that their sufferings can serve as a pertinent example of the oppression of Palestinians by

Israeli military forces, an oppression that continues, quite unabated, since the initiation of the peace process.

GEOGRAPHY AND BACKGROUND

As we mentioned in our Newsletter No. 16, the Gaza Strip is approximately 46 kilometers long. It is 12.5 kilometers wide at its southern end and 7 kilometers wide at its northern end. To the north and east the Gaza Strip borders Israel. To the south it borders Egypt. To the west is the Mediterranean Sea. The Gaza Strip is surrounded by a high fence which day and night is patrolled and guarded on the northern and eastern borders by Israeli troops, and by Egyptian and Israeli soldiers on the southern border. The Mediterranean Sea off the coast of the Gaza Strip is daily and nightly patrolled by Israeli Dabur gunboats.

In the 1993 Oslo Peace Accord it was agreed that until the final settlement, which will bring peace between Israel and the Palestinians, Israel is in charge of external security in the Occupied Territories as well as the security of the Israeli settlers who reside in the Gaza Strip. One result of this agreement was that Gazan fishing boats were allowed to fish in a very restricted zone. That zone was designated Fishing Zone L. It extended twenty nautical miles into the sea opposite the Gaza Strip. (One nautical mile is equal to 6,080 feet, or 1.852 kilometers.) Fishing Zone L was bordered to the north by Closed Area K, whose width was 1.5 nautical miles. There was also Closed Area M, whose width was one nautical mile, to the south of Fishing Zone L. These border areas in the sea were part of the legal waters of the Gaza Strip. In short, for so-called security reasons, the Oslo Agreement limited the area in which Gazan fisherman were allowed to fish. Fishermen from the Gaza Strip were not allowed to enter the closed areas.

The official reason for the closed areas of the sea opposite the Gaza Strip was to not allow Palestinian terrorists to use the sea to infiltrate Israel or Palestinian smugglers to smuggle goods. A secondary reason was to not allow fishing boats from the Gaza Strip to stray over the border to Israeli waters in the north or to Egyptian waters in the south. Let us say immediately that in the seven years since the signing of the agreement, the Israeli navy and army have not reported one incident of terrorist activity that used a fishing boat from Gaza. Nor has it reported one instance of smuggling of goods by a fishing boat from Gaza.

These facts are important, hence we emphasize them. In many dozens, if not hundreds, of incidents in which the Israeli navy searched, arrested, and harassed Palestinian fishermen during the past seven years, they never found firearms or other weapons on the Palestinian boats. Nor did they ever find contraband. Yet the Israeli army continues to state that there are grave suspicions that the Gazan fishing boats engage in terrorist activities or smuggling. In a word, the Israeli army spokespersons are deceiving the public.

COMPLAINTS BY FISHERMEN OF GAZA

Here are three complaints of harassment by the Israeli navy that were presented to us by fishermen from Gaza. During the winter and spring of 2000, we sent these complaints, together with eighteen similar complaints, to the Israeli army spokesperson. Her answers will be briefly described after the complaints.

COMPLAINT OF ABED ISA ABED ALRAHMAN ALWAN, ID #937650275. BOAT #30016. FISHERMAN LICENSE #3-18031

My boat is a launch, 13 meters long and 4.5 meters wide. I fish for sardines. On May 27, 1998, at 7:00 P.M, together with eight other fishermen, I sailed from the Khan Yunis port. To my launch, I attached two small boats, with a fisherman in each boat. About an hour later, when we were around eight miles from the shore, an Israeli Dabur gunboat approached us. They approached the small boats. We fishermen in the launch approached the Dabur and asked what they wanted. In response, they opened fire on us. It was dark and I could not see what weapon was firing at us. Later we found thirty-six bullet holes in the launch and additional bullet holes in one of the small boats, which later was sunk. They also threw a grenade whose purpose was to stun us. They then sent out a rope and circular hook, which at the second try caught our launch and pulled it aside the Dabur gunboat.

The Israeli sailors tied the launch to the Dabur and, under threats of their guns, pulled us south to Closed Area M, where fishing is not allowed. Once they reached Closed Area M, they photographed us in the area; from the flashes of the camera, we understood that we were being photographed. They then sailed north with us, to the Israeli port of Ashdod. There were eight sailors on the Dabur, and they forced four of us, including myself, to come aboard the gunboat. The sailors blindfolded the four of us with sacks over our heads and tied us to the rail on the side of the Dabur. They then started to beat us with the stocks of their rifles. They took a stick with nails in it and beat my son so much that he lost consciousness. We sailed thus for four hours, and all the time they cursed us and periodically renewed beating us.

When we reached Ashdod, the sailors took the sacks off our heads and untied us. An ambulance came and took my unconscious son on a stretcher to some place—we were not told where he was taken. The sailors searched the launch and found nothing but fishing nets and ropes. We were taken to be interrogated. The interrogator, who spoke Arabic, did not know why we had been brought to him. He called and asked an Israeli commander at the military port why we had been arrested. They told him that it was a mistake. The interrogator told me and the other fishermen that we had been arrested by mistake and that in an hour we would be returned to the Gaza Strip.

After an hour the Dabur gunboat, with us on board, started to sail back to the Gaza Strip pulling my launch and the two small boats. The Dabur suddenly started to sail very quickly and in zigzags. As a result the two small boats sunk. I asked the Israeli sailors to stop sailing so quickly and help us pull out the sunken boats. In response the sailors beat us with the stocks of their rifles and cut the rope to my two boats, so that they could not be retrieved. They ridiculed us and said: "When you reach Gaza, Arafat will give you the two boats." When I asked them for water to drink, one sailor went aside, pissed into a bottle, and gave it to me to drink. I smelled the urine in the bottle and threw it into the sea, and he then hit me again with the stock of his rifle. One sailor went into my launch with an ax and started hitting the motor, demolishing it; he also spilled the oil. We finally reached Palestinian waters where the Palestine Marine Police waited for us. My son has been suffering from trauma ever since and cannot work. A seventy-year-old fisherman who was with us has also suffered from trauma and cannot work. That night the Israelis destroyed $40,000 of equipment, and I have not yet been able to raise the money to return to fishing. The group of fishermen who worked with me support forty people and are out of work. The first year of our being unemployed we received support from UNRWA.

COMPLAINT OF NAFEZ ALI MACHMUD ZHALACH, I.D. #956515548. BOAT #G-306. FISHERMAN LICENSE #101311

On November 12, 1994, at 9:00 P.M. I and my brother Ramda were fishing eight sea miles off the shore, west of Sedonia—which is definitely in area L—when we were suddenly approached by an Israeli Dabur gunboat; its number was 853. An Israeli sailor said to us: "It is forbidden to be here; go back 500 meters." I asked him to allow me half an hour to pick up my fishing net from the sea, and then I would go back. The Israeli sailors refused and ordered me to cut the net. The sailors then ordered me to give them everything that was in the boat. I did. They then notified my brother and me that we were arrested and they would take us with our boat to Ashdod port. But, instead of arresting us they began shooting my boat, which was ten meters from the Dabur. Three sailors began shooting with M16s to the front of my boat, to prevent me from going back to Gaza. They shot at least 300 bullets into my boat and damaged its front. A ricochet penetrated my brother's head. While the Israelis gave my brother first aid, I was standing up on my boat. Suddenly something massive was shot at my boat, and it began sinking. The soldiers threw to me a lifesaver and hauled me onto the Dabur. They tied my legs, and tied my hands behind my back. They did the same to my brother. I asked them why they were treating us in this manner: "Am I a dog?" The soldiers answered: "This is war behavior." They took us to Ashdod port, and there a medical doctor checked us and took care of my wounded brother.

During the investigation, I was asked about the price of the boat and the property that was on it. I answered that the boat cost $3,000; its engine cost

$3,000; the fishing net cost $1,000; the fish were also worth around $1,000. The total sum was $8,000 dollars. The investigator made note of all this. After the investigation we were released. My brother had to stay at home for three months because of the wound in his head, his shock and trauma, his physical imbalance, and the fears he had after this event. The Israelis did not compensate me for my loss, and I have gone to court.

COMPLAINT OF HALIL ABED ABDALLA BARDUIL, I.D. #920618048. BOAT #4-14-5.

On or around May 6, 2000, at 11:00 A.M., I went to fish with my Hassake [small boat], using my Chinchila net, together with four other fishermen. At a distance of about two kilometers from Rafah shore, in Fishing Zone L, I spread the net in circular form around a group of fish. After the net sank, we began to raise it up with the fish that were caught in it. Suddenly an Israeli Dabur gunboat approached us; on it were five sailors and an officer. Its number was 905. The officer did not ask for a permit and did not say to us anything. One of the sailors took an iron stick with a big hook, whose length was more than five meters, and he began to pull my net up from the sea. After he picked up part of the net, he tied it to the Dabur, and they began to sail backwards with great force. They tore more than eighty meters of my net. The fish that were inside the net either died or escaped. In addition, I lost 700 small buoys that were tied to the net. The total damage is more than $6,000.

THE RESPONSE OF THE ARMY SPOKESPERSON

From January to June, 2000, we sent twenty-one complaints, including the three cited above, to the Israeli navy and the army spokesperson. In response to all the specific complaints, we received a two-page reply, most of it general statements and superficial, vague assertions about how the Israeli and Palestinian authorities work together. The spokesperson's response did not address any of the above three complaints. It did address very partially and vaguely three other complaints, without answering whether the Israeli navy had found anyone guilty of harassing the Palestinians. We found this response totally unsatisfactory, and in a seven-page, detailed letter asked the army spokesperson to fully answer all of the fishermen's complaints in full detail.

In addition, we asked the Moked, an Israeli human rights organization, to help the fishermen. They agreed, and their lawyer has sent four of the twenty-one complaints of the fishermen, which are similar to the above cited complaints, to the navy's legal counsel, asking for his response. If the response is not favorable, and if the fishermen are not compensated for their losses and their personal suffering, the Moked lawyer will take the navy to court and ask that the court force the Israeli navy to compensate the four fishermen for their losses and their suffering. According to the response of the navy to these four complaints, the lawyer from Moked will decide how to deal with the other seventeen complaints. Needless to say, all of this legal negotiation and work will take much time.

SUMMARY

From our brief presentation, it is evident that during the past seven years, the so-called peace process between Israel and the Palestinian Authority has not benefited the fishermen in the Gaza Strip, most of whom live in refugee camps. Two additional simple facts show the sad truth of this statement. The first is that the number of registered fishermen in the Gaza Strip during these past seven years has declined from 4,105 fishermen before the Oslo Agreement in 1993 to 3,353 fishermen today. The catch that all the fishermen in the Gaza Strip bring home has also declined, by about 25 percent. Much of this decline in the number of fishermen and in their catch is a result of Israel's harsh and unjust policies.

However, this ongoing oppression of the fishermen in the Gaza Strip must be viewed from a broader perspective. The oppression of the fishermen clearly indicates that in many areas of Palestinian life, the so-called peace process partially served as a cover-up for Israeli forces continuing the harsh and unjust oppression and the brutal exploitation of the Palestinians in the Gaza Strip.

Today, there are still many areas of Palestinian daily life in which oppression and exploitation are manifested—from the cheating of Palestinian laborers in Israel, to poor health care, violation of human rights, and from the difficulty of shipping Palestinian goods out of Gaza, to lack of freedom of movement of 70 percent of the residents of the Gaza Strip. This oppression and exploitation has been very much ignored in the Israeli press, by Israeli intellectuals, and by so-called peace workers—many of whom hide under the cover of their support for the peace process.

For instance, according to the Israeli press, the current government minister and former prime minister, Shimon Peres, who received the Nobel Peace Prize, has established an institute for Palestinian-Israeli peace. In a fit of modesty, Shimon Peres called his institute The Peres Institute for Peace. This institute has a yearly budget of millions of dollars. Since its inception five years ago, the Peres Institute for Peace has not once published a single statement that addressed the ongoing suffering of the Palestinians in the Gaza Strip—suffering that continued during the seven years of the peace process.

This ongoing oppression and exploitation of the Palestinians in the Gaza Strip and the West Bank, under the veil of the peace process, is also ruinous for Israeli democracy. A democracy must be based on a truthful approach to the matters at hand. Deceit corrodes the trust that citizens give to democratic institutions. In the past seven years, it is most unfortunate that Israeli leaders have embraced the policy of oppressing and exploiting the Palestinians, and ignoring their human rights, while declaring that they are in the midst of a peace process which, so far, has not brought peace and freedom to the Palestinian people.

Further Reading

Arendt, Hannah. *Between Past and Future: Eight Exercises in Political Thought.* Middlesex, England: Penguin Books, 1977.

Atik, Naim Stifan. *Justice and Only Justice: A Palestinian Theology of Liberation.* Maryknoll, NY: Orbis Books, 1989.

Atik, Naim Stifan, Marc H. Ellis, and Rosemary Rathford Reuther, eds. *Faith and Intifada: Palestinian Christian Voices.* Maryknoll, NY: Orbis Books, 1992.

Ben-Dor, Gabriel, ed. *The Palestinians and the Middle East Conflict.* Ramat Gan: Turtledove Publishing, 1978.

Berque, Jacques. *Arab Rebirth: Pain and Ecstasy.* London: Al Saqi Books, 1983.

Boulding, Elise, ed. *Building Peace in the Middle East: Challenges for States and Civil Society.* Boulder, CO: Lynne Rienner Publishers, 1994.

Buber, Martin. *I and Thou.* Translated by Ronald Gregor Smith. New York: Scribner's, 1958.

Chomsky, Noam. *Necessary Illusions: Thought Control in Democratic Societies.* Boston MA: South End Press, 1989.

———. *World Orders, Old and New.* London: Pluto Press, 1994.

———. *Powers and Prospects.* Boston: South End Press, 1996.

Cohen, Akiba A., and Gadi Wolfsfeld, eds. *Framing the Intifada: People and Media.* Norwood, NJ: Ablex Publishing, 1993.

Donohue, John J., and John L. Esposito, eds. *Islam in Transition: Muslim Perspectives.* Oxford: Oxford University Press, 1982.

Gazit, Shlomo. *The Carrot and the Stick: Israel's Policy in Judea and Samaria, 1967–1968.* Washington, DC: B'nai B'rith Books, 1985.

Gordon, Haim. *Dance, Dialogue, and Despair: Existentialist Philosophy and Education for Peace in Israel.* Tuscaloosa: University of Alabama Press, 1986.

———. *Make Room for Dreams: Spiritual Challenges to Zionism.* Westport, CT: Greenwood Press, 1989.

———. *Quicksand: Israel, the Intifada and the Rise of Political Evil in Democracies.* East Lansing: Michigan State University Press, 1995.

———, ed. *Looking Back at the June 1967 War.* Westport, CT: Praeger, 1999.

Gordon, Haim, and Rivca Gordon, eds. *Israel/Palestine: The Quest for Dialogue*. Mary-knoll, NY: Orbis Books, 1991.

———. *Sartre and Evil: Guidelines for a Struggle*. Westport, CT: Greenwood Press, 1995.

Gordon, Neve, and Ruchama Marton, eds. *Torture, Human Rights, Medical Ethics and the Case of Israel*. London: Zed Books, 1995.

Harkabi, Yehoshafat. *The Palestinian Covenant and Its Meaning*. London: Vallentine Mitchell, 1979.

Hass, Amira. *Drinking the Sea at Gaza* (in Hebrew). Tel Aviv: The New Library, 1996.

Heikal, Mohamed. *The Sphinx and the Commisar: The Rise and Fall of Soviet Influence in the Middle East*. New York: Harper and Row, 1978.

Inbari, Pinhas. *The Palestinians: Between Terrorism and Statehood*. Brighton, England: Sussex Academic Press, 1996.

Isaac J., and H. Shuval, eds. *Water and Peace in the Middle East*. Amsterdam: Elsevier, 1994.

Langer, Felicia. *An Age of Stone*. Translated by Isaac Cohen. London: Quartet Books, 1988.

Lukacs, Yehuda, ed. *Documents on the Israeli-Palestinian Conflict, 1967–1983*. Cambridge: Cambridge University Press, 1984.

Mendes-Flohr, Paul R. *A Land of Two People: Martin Buber on Jews and Arabs*. Oxford: Oxford University Press, 1983.

Morris, Benny. *The Birth of the Palestinian Refugee Problem, 1947–1949*. Cambridge: Cambridge University Press, 1987.

———. *1948 and After: Israel and the Palestinians*. Oxford: Oxford University Press, 1994.

Nassar, Jamal R. and Roger Heacock, eds. *Intifada: Palestine at the Crossroads*. New York: Praeger, 1990.

Pappe, Ilan, ed. *The Israel/Palestine Question*. London: Routledge, 1999.

Peretz, Don. *The West Bank: History, Politics, Society, and Economics*. Boulder, CO: Westview Press, 1986.

Rosenthal, Ruvik. *Kafr Kassem: Myth and Reality* (in Hebrew). Tel Aviv: Hakibbutz Hameuchad Publishing House, 2000.

Roy, Sara. *The Gaza Strip: The Political Economy of De-development*. Washington, DC: Institute for Palestine Studies, 1995.

Shalev, Aryeh. *The Intifada: Causes and Effects* (in Hebrew). Tel Aviv: Papyrus Publishing House, 1990.

Shif, Zeev and Ehud Y'ari. *Intifada* (in Hebrew). Tel Aviv: Schocken Publishing House, 1990.

Tacitus. *The Agricola and The Germania*. Translated by H. Mattingly and S. A. Handford. London: Penguin Books, 1970.

Vatikiotis, P.J. *The History of Egypt: From Muhammad Ali to Mubarak*. London: Weidenfeld and Nicolson, 1985.

Index

About the Authors

HAIM GORDON is Professor of Education at Ben Gurion University, Beer Sheva, Israel. He is the editor, coeditor, or author of 17 earlier books.

RIVCA GORDON is the Director of the Foundation for Democratic Education in Israel and is an independent scholar who has coauthored or edited several earlier books.

TAHER SHRITEH is a freelance journalist who has worked for CBS, BBC, the *New York Times*, and Reuters in the Gaza Strip.